RABBI MOSES

A Documentary Catalogue

Jacob Neusner

Studies in Judaism

University Press of America,® Inc.
Lanham · Boulder · New York · Toronto · Plymouth, UK

Copyright © 2013 by
University Press of America,® Inc.
4501 Forbes Boulevard
Suite 200
Lanham, Maryland 20706
UPA Acquisitions Department (301) 459-3366

10 Thornbury Road
Plymouth PL6 7PP
United Kingdom

All rights reserved
Printed in the United States of America
British Library Cataloging in Publication Information Available

Library of Congress Control Number: 2013930465
ISBN: 978-0-7618-6091-4 (paperback : alk. paper)
eISBN: 978-0-7618-6092-1

™The paper used in this publication meets the minimum requirements of American National Standard for Information Sciences—Permanence of Paper for Printed Library Materials, ANSI Z39.48-1992

Studies in Judaism

EDITOR

Jacob Neusner
Bard College

EDITORIAL BOARD

Alan J. Avery-Peck
College of the Holy Cross

Herbert Basser
Queens University

Bruce D. Chilton
Bard College

José Faur
Bar Ilan University

William Scott Green
University of Miami

Mayer Gruber
Ben-Gurion University of the Negev

Günter Stemberger
University of Vienna

James F. Strange
University of South Florida

Contents

Preface vii

Introduction xi

1. Moses in the Mishnah and Abot 1
2. Moses in the Tosefta 7
3. Moses in Sifra 13
4. Moses in Sifré to Numbers and Sifré Zutta to Numbers 15
5. Moses in Sifré to Deuteronomy 19
6. Moses in Mekhilta Attributed to R. Ishmael 27
7. Moses in Genesis Rabbah 37
8. Moses in Leviticus Rabbah 43
9. Moses in Pesiqta Derab Kahana 47
10. Moses in Esther Rabbah I 53
11. Moses in Song of Songs Rabbah 55
12. Moses in Ruth Rabbah 57
13. Moses in Lamentations Rabbah 61
14. Moses in the Fathers According to Rabbi Nathan 71
15. Moses in Yerushalmi Berakhot and Zeraim 85
16. Moses in Yerushalmi Moed 89
17. Moses in Yerushalmi Nashim 97
18. Moses in Yerushalmi Neziqin 99
19. Moses in Bavli Berakhot 103
20. Moses in Bavli Moed 107
21. Moses in Bavli Nashim 115
22. Moses in Bavli Neziqin, Bavli Sanhedrin 119
23. Moses in Bavli Qodoshim and Niddah 123
24. Moses as a Figure in the Documentary Catalogue 127

Preface

This is an exercise in the systematic recourse to anachronism as a theological-exegetical mode of apologetics. Specifically I demonstrate the capacity of the Rabbinic sages to read ideas attested in their own day as authoritative testaments to — to them — ancient times. So the role of anachronism knew no limits, and Scripture was read as integral testimony to the contemporary scene.

The Rabbinic sages in the fourth and fifth centuries C. E. represented by the Mishnah and the Talmud possess in Scriptures from remote antiquity a heritage filled with contradictions. That imperfection from ancient times challenges the new generations. That is to seek harmony where the clash of opinion yielded flaws. The quest for perfection signaled by the absence of contradiction defines the long history of Judaism.

About a millennium — 750 B.C. E. to 350 C. E. — separates Scripture's prophets from the later sages of the Mishnah and the Talmud. It is quite natural to recognize evidence for differences over a long period of time. Yet Judaism sees itself as a continuum and overcomes difference. The late-comers portray the ancients like themselves. "In our image, after our likeness" captures the current aspiration. The sages accommodated the later documents in their canon by finding the traits of their own time in the record of the remote in past. They met the challenges to perfection the repertoire of the sages in their encounter with the prophets

Of what does the process of harmonization consist? To answer that question I survey the presentation of the prophets by the rabbis, beginning with Moses. To overcome the gap Rabbinic sages turn Moses into a sage like themselves. The prophet performs wonders. The sage sets forth reasonable rulings. In Chapter Twenty-four I expand on this account of matters to show the categorical solution that the sages adopted for themselves, and that is the outcome of the study.

I plan to carry forward the issues of this and a number of prior monographs and consider other figures of interest to Scripture and to Rabbinic sources. The translations are my own.

Jeremiah in Talmud and Midrash. A Source Book. Lanham, 2006: University Press of America STUDIES IN JUDAISM SERIES

Rabbi Jeremiah. Lanham, 2006: University Press of America STUDIES IN JUDAISM SERIES

Amos in Talmud and Midrash. A Source Book. Lanham, 2007: University Press of America STUDIES IN JUDAISM SERIES

Hosea in Talmud and Midrash. A Source Book. Lanham, 2007: University Press of America STUDIES IN JUDAISM SERIES

Micah and Joel in Talmud and Midrash. A Source Book. Lanham, 2007: University Press of America STUDIES IN JUDAISM SERIES

Habakkuk, Jonah, Nahum, and Obadiah in Talmud and Midrash. A Source Book. Lanham, 2007: University Press of America STUDIES IN JUDAISM SERIES

Zephaniah, Haggai, Zechariah, and Malachi in Talmud and Midrash. A Source Book. Lanham, 2007: University Press of America STUDIES IN JUDAISM SERIES

Ezekiel in Talmud and Midrash. A Source Book. Lanham, 2007: University Press of America STUDIES IN JUDAISM SERIES

Isaiah in Talmud and Midrash. A Source Book. A. Mishnah, Tosefta, Tannaite Midrash-Compilations, Yerushalmi and Associated Midrash-Compilations. Lanham, 2007: University Press of America STUDIES IN JUDAISM SERIES.

Isaiah in Talmud and Midrash. A Source Book. B. The Later Midrash-Compilations and the Bavli. Lanham, 2007: University Press of America STUDIES IN JUDAISM SERIES.

The Rabbis, the Law, and the Prophets, Lanham, 2007: University Press of America STUDIES IN JUDAISM SERIES

Rabbinic Theology and Israelite Prophecy. Primacy of the Torah, Narrative of the World to Come, Doctrine of Repentance and Atonement, and the Systematization of Theology in the Rabbis' Reading of the Prophets Lanham, 2007: University Press of America STUDIES IN JUDAISM SERIES.

Rabbi David. A Documentary Catalogue. Lanham, 2012: University Press of America

Preface

My thanks go to Bard College for longtime support of my research and to Professor Bruce Chilton for sharing his erudition and insight,

JACOB NEUSNER

DISTINGUISHED SERVICE PROFESSOR OF THE HISTORY AND THEOLOGY OF JUDAISM
SENIOR FELLOW, INSTITUTE OF ADVANCED THEOLOGY
BARD COLLEGE
ANNANDALE-ON-HUDSON, NEW YORK, 12504

NEUSNER@BARD.EDU

In these pages I survey the ways in which the Rabbinic documents mediate the Scripture's statements to their own times.

Introduction

At issue is the relationship between two kindred Judaic systems of religious thought, the Rabbinic, represented by the Mishnah, Talmuds and Midrash of the first six centuries of the Common Era, and the Prophetic, represented by Moses in the Torah written six hundred years B. C. E. Comparing the figure of Moses in two bodies of writing aims at affording perspective on the character of the second of the two systems, Rabbinic Judaism in its established context of continuity with Scripture. A formal continuity is signaled in the provision of scriptural proof-texts over and over again.

On the surface what singles out Rabbinic writings is the constant recourse to Scripture for proof-texts, bearing the implicit claim to represent the received revelation. But what of the substance of matters? Here through implicit comparison and contrast we test that Rabbinic claim of continuity with Scripture against the datum of Prophecy. We take up categories of theology yielded by Moses's diverse and diffuse statements and compare those categories with the positions taken in the Rabbinic canon of late antiquity by the ancient Rabbinic sages — thus, systemic comparison.

Why speak of comparing *systems of thought*, not just setting in array a host of random parallels one by one — free-floating sentences or random sentiments? Singleton verses of a Prophetic writing do, after all, intersect here and there with singleton statements of Talmudic Rabbis. But the stakes in this book are different. I aim at showing continuities of thought and proposition, not merely careful paraphrase of the received text. I hold that Moses and the Rabbinic sages responded in the same way to the same sort of crisis. At issue is theology, not culture.

Precisely how do the Rabbis of the formative canon naturalize Moses to their system and thus Rabbinize Prophecy? It represents the outcome of a categorical exercise that the outcome was fixed. In taking over the heritage of ancient Israelite Prophecy and law, have the Rabbis subverted Prophecy's religious vision or adapted and adopted it, making that vision their own? By identifying the principal propositions of the Prophet and by examining both the Rabbinic reading of the Prophet and the Rabbinic theology of those same propositions, I answer that question.

What I want to know is two things.

First, in what ways did the ancient Rabbis absorb Moses into their system, naturalize him as a Rabbi, thus "Rabbi Moses"?

Second, I ask whether and how the Rabbinic system responded not only in detail but systematically to Moses, also read as a coherent statement?

The answer to these questions presents itself in the collection of cases that make up the bulk of this book.

It is a commonplace that the Rabbis Rabbinized the received writings of ancient Israel. Anachronism characterized their historical writing. That is commonplace. What is jarring is that we shall see Moses, like other Prophets such as Isaiah, explicitly called a Rabbi. He is the product of a categorical construction, and we shall see the categories of sage and prophet in play throughout the canon. I demonstrate beyond doubt the power of categorization of sage and holy man. What matters here is what the Rabbinic writers meant by that characterization. Exactly how did these processes of Rabbinization produce the outcome a system we may call Prophetic-Rabbinic, not merely how they yielded nothing more than anachronism.

I therefore compare principal theological propositions of Moses with principal propositions on the same issues of the Rabbinic theological system. The reason for attempting systemic comparison is compelling. The Rabbinic writings constitute not arbitrary compilations of odds and ends but coherent expositions of bodies of ideas, sets of theological propositions that hold together. They form legal norms that are principled and that exhibit cogency. The Prophets for their part set forth not only ad hoc words of exhortation and admonition but doctrines that infuse their Prophecies. In both cases therefore we deal with more than random collections of sayings or rules. What we shall see is how the Rabbinic system took over and made its own the Prophetic one. What we shall investigate is whether that process of accommodation followed the main lines of system and thought of the Prophet subject to Rabbinic adaptation.

In examining the bulk of references to Moses in the Rabbinic canon, I follow a simple repertoire of questions. These emerge from the program of definition that animates the inquiry document by document.

[1] Is Moses an active player or a routine and scarcely animate one? The Rabbinic sages represent sages in both manners, sometimes as the exemplary and original actor and sometimes as a routine example of a fixed rule. How are matters with Moses in the successive documents, and do we discern shifts from document to document?

[2] What components of the collection make routine glosses of the received Scriptures and which ones provide more than minor glosses of the tradition?

[3] Can we identify a pronounced bias or a polemical program in the unfolding entries that transform Moses king of Israel into Rabbi Moses Or are the entries that clarify Scripture through the contrast with tradition scattered without pattern in the Rabbinic canon?

[4] How is Moses comparable to sages in this document? How else may we classify the figure of Moses if not as a sage in this document?

Joining "Rabbi" and "Moses" in making a catalogue of the references to Moses in the late antique Rabbinic documents, which is what I do in these pages

Introduction

form Chapter One through Chapter Twenty-Three, yields an oxymoron. That is "Rabbi + Moses." Moses in Scripture is not described in the way rabbis are described in the documents in which they occur at all. If "rabbi" then — how come Moses? And if Moses, then whence rabbi? Scripture's Moses was no sage, and no sage in the Mishnah or the Tosefta was celebrated as the prophet. Moses becomes "our rabbi" only in the later documents of classical Judaism. The components of the formative canon of Rabbinic Judaism — the Mishnah for example — know no sage called "Rabbi Moses" or "Moses our rabbi."

I omit reference to Moses in one aspect. I do not catalogue neutral or conventional references to the Torah of Moses. I underline a case to show the obvious as in the following:

Mishnah Yoma

3:8 A. He came over to his bullock.
B. Now his bullock was set between the Porch and the Altar
C. Its head was to the south and its face to the west.
D. And the priest stands at the east, with his face to the west.
E. And he puts his two hands on it and states the confession.
F. And thus did he say, "O Lord, I have committed iniquity, transgressed, and sinned before you, I and my house. O Lord, forgive the iniquities, transgressions, and sins, which I have done by committing iniquity, transgression, and sin before you, I and my house.
G. "<u>As it is written in the Torah of Moses, your servant</u>, For on this day shall atonement be made for you to clean you. From all your sins shall you be clean before the Lord (Lev. 16:30)."
H. And they respond to him, "Blessed is the name of the glory of his kingdom forever and ever."

"The Torah of Moses" here is a theological cliché and does not bear a polemical charge. This exercise thus continues a planned series of studies of how the ancient Rabbis of the formative age of Judaism, the first six centuries C.E., represented by the Mishnah, Midrash, and Talmuds received and responded to the Prophets of ancient Israel: the Rabbinization of Prophecy. The project does not promise to contribute to scholarship on Moses and claims only to give a fair summary of the main points made by his writings. What we earn here concerns Rabbinic Judaism, not the historical Moses. At issue is the relationship of Rabbinic Judaism to a formidable part of its Scriptural heritage.

The theology of Talmudic law and lore has been set forth, for the Aggadah, in my *The Theology of the Oral Torah. Revealing the Justice of God*. Kingston and Montreal, 1999: McGill-Queen's University Press, and for the Halakhah in *The Halakhah: An Encyclopaedia of the Law of Judaism*. Leiden, 1999: E. J. Brill I-V, and also *The Theology of the Halakhah*. Leiden, 2001: E. J. Brill.

Scriptural translations in general follow Herbert G. May and Bruce M. Metzger, eds., *The Oxford Annotated Bible with the Apocrypha. Revised Standard Version* (N.Y., 1965: Oxford University Press).

My tedious assembly of references to Moses document by document thus aims at a specific goal. Each chapter takes up allusions to Moses in a particular document. I survey the greater part of the references to Moses in the Rabbinic canon but omit some of the more trivial allusions. I present the outcome of my survey of a particular document at the outset and then review the references to Moses in a particular document.

1

Moses in the Mishnah and Abot

The Mishnah invokes scriptural facts and also introduces Rabbinic concepts into its exposition and extension of those facts. Moses is portrayed as law giver and occasionally as prophet. Reference is made to laws given to Moses at Mount Sinai and handed on as oral tradition from there. That is the principal Rabbinic conception and marks Moses in the Mishnah as a typical rabbi.

M. Parah 3:5

A. "[If] they did not find [the residue of the ash] from seven [former cows of purification], they did it from six, from five, from four, from three, from two, from one.
B. "And who prepared them?
C. "The first did Moses prepare. And the second did Ezra prepare.
D. "And five from Ezra onward," the words of R. Meir.
E. And sages say, "Seven from Ezra onward. And who prepared them? Simeon the Righteous and Yohanan the High Priest did two each. Elyehoenai b. Haqqof and Hanamel the Egyptian, and Ishmael b. Phiabi did one each."

Moses is a routine figure and supplies a standard case for a catalogue of like cases. Moses is not accorded greater authority than any other sage. The mark of the rabbinical Moses is his matching the patterns inaugurated by other rabbis. He has no power to exercise differently from other rabbis.

[1] Is Moses an active player or a routine and scarcely animate one? Moses is party to a list of those who prepared the red cow. That represents a minority opinion of Meir vs. Sages.

[2] What components of the collection make routine glosses of the received Scriptures and which ones provide more than minor glosses of the tradition? Moses in the Mishnah is a routine figure.

[3] Can we identify a pronounced bias or a polemical program in the unfolding entries that transform Moses king of Israel into Rabbi Moses? Or are the entries that clarify Scripture through the contrast with tradition scattered without pattern in the Rabbinic canon? I detect no evidence of the recognition of Rabbi Moses as a distinct person.

[4] How is Moses comparable to sages in this document? How else may we classify the figure of Moses if not as a sage in this document? Moses is comparable merely to Ezra and Yohanan the High Priest. Moses is a routine figure,

M Peah 2:6

A. M'SH R. Simeon of Mispah sowed [his field with two types of wheat].
B. [The matter came] before Rabban Gamaliel. So they went up to the Chamber of Hewn Stone, and asked [about the law regarding sowing two types of wheat in one field].
C. Said Nahum the Scribe, "I have received [the following ruling] from R. Miasha, who received [it] from his father, who received [it] from the Pairs, who received [it] from the Prophets, [who received] the law [given] to Moses on Sinai, regarding one who sows his field with two types of wheat:
D. "If he harvests [the wheat] in one lot, he designates one [portion of produce as] peah.
E. "If he harvests [the wheat] in two lots, he designates two [portions of produce as] peah."

Moses sets forth law given by God at Mt. Sinai. The law treats a minor detail and does not invoke prophetic morality. Moses is a master of the law, not a prophetic figure.

[1] Moses stands in the chain of tradition beginning at Sinai.

[2] What components of the collection make routine glosses of the received Scriptures and which ones provide more than minor glosses of the tradition? A contribution to the chain of tradition commencing at Sinai surely qualifies as a major component of the tradition of Moses. This signifies as a major tradition.

[3] Can we identify a pronounced bias or a polemical program in the unfolding entries that transform Moses king of Israel into Rabbi Moses? The Mishnah knows the tradition of Moses at Sinai and takes an active role in invoking that tradition.

[4] How is Moses comparable to sages in this document? Moses stands in the tradition of oral revelation of Sinai. How else may we classify the figure of Moses if not as a sage in this document? Moses is comparable to any rabbi. The Mishnah is classified as a Rabbinic document.

1. Moses in the Mishnah and Abot

Mishnah Rosh Hashanah 2:9

A. Said to him Rabban Gamaliel, "I decree that you come to me with your staff and purse on the Day of Atonement which is determined in accord with your reckoning."

B. R. Aqiba went and found him troubled.

C. He said to him, "I can provide grounds for showing that everything that Rabban Gamaliel has done is validly done, since it says, 'These are the set feasts of the Lord, even holy convocations, which you shall proclaim' (Lev. 23:4) Whether they are in their proper time or not in their proper time, I have no set feasts but these [which you shall proclaim] [vs. M. 2:7D]."

D. He came along to R. Dosa b. Harkinas.

E. He [Dosa] said to him, "Now if we're going to take issue with the court of Rabban Gamaliel, we have to take issue with every single court which has come into being from the time of Moses to the present day,

F. "since it says, Then went up Moses and Aaron, Nadab and Abihu, and seventy of the elders of Israel (Ex . 24:9).

G. "Now why have the names of the elders not been given? To teach that every group of three [elders] who came into being as a court of Israel — lo, they are equivalent to the court of Moses himself."

H. [Joshua] took his staff with his purse in his hand and went along to Yabneh, to Rabban Gamaliel, on the Day of Atonement which is determined in accord with his [Gamaliel's] reckoning.

I. Rabban Gamaliel stood up and kissed him on his head and said to him, "Come in peace, my master and my disciple —

J. "My master in wisdom, and my disciple in accepting my rulings."

[1] Is Moses an active player or a routine and scarcely animate one? Moses is a conventional figure, participating in a tradition. The [point of the story is that the Rabbinic tradition governs and requires the subservience of the sages. That point I heavily emphasized and leaves no marks of a unique figure

[2] What components of the collection make routine glosses of the received Scriptures and which ones provide more than minor glosses of the tradition? Moses as judge is a routine figure.

[3] Can we identify a pronounced bias or a polemical program in the unfolding entries that transform Moses the prophet and king of Israel into Rabbi Moses? Or are the entries that clarify Scripture through the contrast with tradition scattered without pattern in the Rabbinic canon? This is Moses as an active figure.

[4] How is Moses comparable to sages in this document? How else may we classify the figure of Moses if not as a sage in this document? Moses is the quintessential sage, a judge in court.

Mishnah Sotah 1:9

A. And so is it on the good side:
B. Miriam waited a while for Moses, since it is said, "And his sister stood afar off (Ex. 2:4), therefore, Israel waited on her seven days in the wilderness, since it is said, "And the people did not travel on until Miriam was brought in again" (Num. 12:15).
C. Joseph had the merit of burying his father, and none of his brothers was greater than he, since it is said (Gen. 50:7,9).
D. We have none so great as Joseph, for only Moses took care of his [bones].
E. Moses had the merit of burying the bones of Joseph, and none in Israel was greater than he, since it is said, "And Moses took the bones of Joseph with him" (Ex. 13:19).
F. We have none so great as Moses, for only the Holy One blessed be He took care of his [bones], since it is said, "And he buried him in the valley" (Dt. 34:6).
G. And not of Moses alone have they stated [this rule], but of all righteous people, since it is said, "And your righteousness shall go before you. "The glory of the Lord shall gather you [in death]" (Is. 58:8).

Moses is a figure on a chain of tradition, model along with other sages, not a unique player different from other rabbis. The active figures are sages in the academy, and Moses is part of the backdrop.

M Eduyyot 8:7

A. Said R. Joshua, "I have a tradition from Rabban Yohanan b. Zakkai, who heard it from his master, and his master from his master, as a law revealed to Moses at Sinai,
B. "that Elijah is not going to come to declare unclean or to declare clean, to put out or to draw near,
C. "but only to put out those who have been brought near by force, and to draw near those who have been put out by force."
D. The family of the house of Seriphah was in Transjordan, and Ben Zion put it out by force.
E. And there was another family there, which Ben Zion drew near by force.
F. It is [families of] this sort that Elijah will come to declare unclean and to declare clean, to put out and to draw near
G. R. Judah says, "To draw near but not to put out."
H. R. Simeon says, "To smooth out disputes."
I. And sages say, "Not to put out or to draw near but to make peace in the world,
J. "as it is said, "Behold I will send you Elijah the prophet and he will return the heart of the fathers to the children, and the heart of the children to the fathers (Ma. 4:23- 24)."

1. Moses in the Mishnah and Abot

Typically for the Mishnah's Moses, Moses is a link in the chain of tradition of Sinai. He is not a prophet but a routine player in the tradition handed on from Sinai.

MISHNAH KETUBOT 7:6

A. And those women go forth without the payment of the marriage contract at all:
B. She who transgresses against the law of Moses and Jewish law.
C. And what is the law of Moses [which she has transgressed]? [If] (1) she feeds him food which has not been tithed, or (2) has sexual relations with him while she is menstruating, or [if] (3) she does not cut off her dough offering, or (4) [if] she vows and does not carry out her vow.

Reference is made to the law of Moses and its contents are invoked. He is a figure in the transmission of the tradition.

TRACTATE ABOT

ABOT 1:1

A. Moses received Torah at Sinai and handed it on to Joshua, Joshua to elders, and elders to prophets,
B. and prophets handed it on to the men of the great assembly.
C. They said three things:

This is a standard claim to the status of Moses as source of Torah-teachings.

ABOT 5:18

A. He who brings merit to the community never causes sin.
B. And he who causes the community to sin — they never give him a sufficient chance to attain penitence.
C. Moses attained merit and bestowed merit on the community.
D. So the merit of the community is assigned to his [credit],
E. as it is said, "He executed the justice of the Lord and his judgments with Israel" (Dt. 33:21).
F. R Jeroboam sinned and caused the community to sin.
G. So the sin of the community is assigned to his [debit],
H. as it is said, "For the sins of Jeroboam which he committed and wherewith he made Israel to sin" (I Kings 15:30).

[1] Is Moses an active player or a routine and scarcely animate one? The Rabbinic sages represent sages in both manners, sometimes as the exemplary and original actor and sometimes as a routine example of a fixed rule. In Abot Moses as revealer of the Torah at Sinai is featured. But Moses is a routine figure and does not initiate important teachings.

[2] What components of the collection make routine glosses of the received Scriptures and which ones provide more than minor glosses of the tradition? Moses stands as a principal figure in the Torah tradition and is a primary example of a sage.

[3] Can we identify a pronounced bias or a polemical program in the unfolding entries that transform Moses king of Israel into Rabbi Moses? We most certainly see Moses as the model for the sage.

[4] How is Moses comparable to sages in this document? How else may we classify the figure of Moses if not as a sage in this document? There is no choice. Moses in the primary document of the Rabbinic canon is identified as a master of the Torah of Sinai oral and written.

The first documents of Rabbinic Judaism — starting with Abot — know the standard traits imputed to Moses as a sage: wonder worker and sage of the law. There is no hint of a conflict between the two pictures of Rabbi Moses. From the beginnings of the Rabbinic writings to the closure of the Rabbinic writings in late antiquity Rabbi Moses appears as a standard Rabbinic figure.

2

Moses in the Tosefta

The Tosefta contains three types of materials: glosses on the Mishnah, which is cited, discussions of the law of the Mishnah, which is not cited in so many words but implicitly, and free-standing statements of rules, which stand apart from the Mishnah's laws.

Tosefta Ketubot 4:9
- A. Hillel the Elder made an exegesis of ordinary language [of legal documents, and not merely of the text of the Torah].
- D. Hillel the elder said to them, "Show me the marriage-contract of your mothers."
- E. They showed them to him, and written in it was the following language:
- F. "When you will enter my house, you will be my wife in accord with the law of Moses and Israel" [but not before that time, on the strength of which he decided that they were not mamzers].

The reference to the "law of Moses" is routine. What follows is the mark of a critical active player, who exemplifies the governing virtue of rabbis.

Tosefta Sotah 4:7
- A. Joseph had the merit of [burying] his father, so it was only Moses who took the trouble to care for his bones, as it is said, And Moses took the bones of Joseph with him (Ex. 13:19) [M. Sot. 1:9C-E].
- B. This teaches that all of the people were occupied with plunder, but he was busy with the doing of a commandment, as it is said, The wise of heart will heed commandments (Prov. 10:8).

The narrative commences with a generalization, a headline for what is to follow. An analytical exposition — "but if not...—" takes over in a large and nuanced exposition. We have a systematic analysis — If Joseph had not taken care of Moses, followed by the secondary inquiry — how did Moses know where Joseph was buried? The Mishnah has nothing to compare with this narrative. The resort to narratives in the exposition of the law is common in the Tosefta and uncommon in the Mishnah. The document imposes its traits on the figure of Moses,

> C. But if Moses had not taken care of him, would the Israelites not have taken care of [Joseph]?
> D. [Yet] Scripture says, "And the bones of Joseph which the children of Israel brought up out of Egypt they buried in Shechem" (Joshua 24:32).
> E. But since the Israelites saw Moses taking care of him, they said, "Leave him be. His [Joseph's] honor will be greater when his rites will be performed by great men rather than by unimportant ones."
> F. Now if Moses and the Israelites had not taken care of [Joseph], would not his own children have taken care of him?
> G. Scripture says, "And they became the inheritance of the children of Joseph" (Joshua 24:32).
> H. But when his children saw Moses and the Israelites taking care of [Joseph], they said, "Leave him be. His [Joseph's] honor will be greater when his rites will be performed by many rather than by few."
> I. How did Moses know where Joseph had been buried?

The extension of the exposition continues in yet another compelling story.

> J. They tell: Serah daughter of Asher was [a survivor] of the generation [of Joseph], and she went and said to Moses, "In the River Nile Joseph is buried. And the Egyptians made for him metal spits and affixed them with pitch [to keep him down]." Moses went and stood at the Nile River and said, "Joseph, the time has come for the Holy One, blessed be He, to redeem Israel.
> "Lo, the Presence is held up for you, and the Israelites are held up for you, and the clouds of glory are held up for you. If you show yourself, well and good, and if not, we are free of the oath which you have imposed upon our fathers."
> K. Then the coffin of Joseph floated to the surface and Moses took it and went his way.
> L. And do not be surprised (that metal should float), for lo, Scripture says, "As one was felling a beam, the axe-head fell into the water ... Alas, my master, for it was borrowed. The man of God said, Where did it fall? And he showed him the place. And he cut down a stick and cast it in, and made the iron to float" (II Kings 6:5-6).
> M. Now is it not a matter of an argument a fortiori.

N. Now if Elisha, disciple of Elijah, disciple of Moses, could do things in such a way, Moses, master of Elijah, master of Elisha, all the more so [should be able to do such things].

O. And some say that Joseph was buried in the royal cemetery, and Moses went and stood at the graves of the kings and said, "Joseph, Joseph! The time has come for the Holy One, blessed be He, to redeem Israel. Lo, the Presence is held up for you, and the Israelites are held up for you and the clouds of glory are held up for you. If you show yourself, well and good, and if not, we are free of the oath which you have imposed upon our fathers."

P. At that moment the coffin of Joseph shook, and Moses took it and went along.

Q. Now there were two coffins traveling with them, one the holy ark, one the ark of the corpse. And everyone who passed by would remark, "What in fact is the character of these two arks?"

R. They would then reply to them, "One is the holy ark, and one is the ark of the corpse."

S. They would say to them, "But is it possible that the holy ark should go along with the ark of a corpse?"

T. They replied, "The corpse which is kept in this ark carried out what is written in that which is lying in the other ark."

TOSEFTA SOTAH 4:8

A. Moses acquired merit [through burying] the bones of Joseph, so only the Omnipresent, blessed be He, took care of him, since it is said, "And he buried him in the valley" (Deut. 34:6) [M. Sot. I:9E-F].

B. This teaches that Moses was laid upon the wings of the Presence for four mils. from the portion of Reuben to the portion of Gad.

C. For he died in the field of a portion of Reuben, but he was buried in a field in the portion of Gad.

D. Now how do we know that he died in the midst of a field of the portion of Reuben? Since it is said, "Ascend this mountain of the Abarim, Mount Nebo" (Deut. 32:49). And Nebo belongs only in the portion of Reuben, as it is said, "And the sons of Reuben built Heshbon, Elealeh, Kiriathaim, Nebo, and Baal-meon" (Num. 33:37-38).

E. Now how do we know that he was buried in a field in the portion of Gad? Since it is said, "And Or Gad he said, Blessed be he who enlarges Gad! Gad couches like a lion, he tears the arm, and the crown of the head. He chose the best of the land for himself, for there a commander's portion was reserved" (Deut. 33:20-21).

[1] Is Moses an active player or a routine and scarcely animate one? That concerns the burial of Joseph when the Israelites left Egypt.

[2] This is more than a minor gloss, it is a principal allegation.

[3] The bias contains the polemic that Moses was the example of generous and responsible conduct.

[4] How is Moses comparable to sages in this document? While the Israelites were engaged in private responsibilities, Moses took the trouble to take are of Joseph's bones. Moses stands for public virtue.

Tosefta Taanit 3:2
A. Eight priestly watches did Moses set up for the priesthood, and eight for the Levites.
B. When David and Samuel, the seer, arose, they divided the priesthood into twenty-four watches, and the Levites into twenty-four watches.

[1] Is Moses an active player or a routine and scarcely animate one? Moses organizes the priestly authorities of the Temple.
[2] This is a minor gloss,
[3] As above,
[4] How is Moses comparable to sages in this document? He is comparable to David and Samuel, not to a sage.

Tosefta Yebamot 8:4
A. A man should not desist from having sexual relations unless he has children [M. Yeb. 6:6A].
B. Grandchildren are deemed [for the purposes of the present rule] to be equivalent to children.
C. [If] one of them died or one of them was made into a eunuch, he then is not permitted to desist from sexual relations.
D. A man has no right to live without a woman, and a woman has no right to live without a man.
E. A man has no right to drink a contraceptive drink so that he should not impregnate a woman,
F. and a woman has no right to drink a contraceptive drink so that she should not become pregnant.
G. A man has no right to marry a barren woman, an old woman, a sterile woman, or a minor, or any who cannot bear children.
H. A woman has no right to be married even to a eunuch [sterile but capable of sexual relations].
I. R. Judah says [regarding D-E], "He who renders males eunuchs is liable [for doing so], but he who does so to females is exempt."
J. R. Nathan says, "The House of Shammai say, 'Two sons — just as Moses had two sons, as it is said, And the sons of Moses, Gershom and Eliezer [I Chron. 23:15].
K. "And the House of Hillel say, 'A son and a daughter, as it is said, Male and female he made them" [M. Yeb. 6:6B-C].

Moses is the model for the law and figures as a minor gloss.

2. Moses in the Tosefta

TOSEFTA BABA MESIA 6:17

- A. Said R. Yosé, "Come and see how blind are the eyes of those who lend at usurious rates.
- I. R. Simeon b. Eleazar says, "More than they make they lose.
- J. "For they treat the Torah like a fraud,
- K. "And Moses like a fool.
- L. "They say, 'Now if Moses knew how much money we would make, he would never have written [the prohibition of usury]!'"

[1] Is Moses an active player or a routine and scarcely animate one? Moses illustrates the law,

[2] Moses is a routine reference point. ?

[3] As above.

[4] Moses is a model.

TOSEFTA BERAKHOT

1:13 "Moses, Moses," "Abraham Abraham," "Jacob Jacob," "Samuel Samuel" [i.e., God's repetition of their names in addressing these men in various scriptural verses] — all these [repetitions] are expressions of endearment, expressions of encouragement, equally applicable before [God] spoke with them and after he spoke with them, before they were appointed to high position and after they were appointed to high position.

Moses is an example along with others to clarify a scriptural usage.

TOSEFTA SANHEDRIN 1:2

- K. "And whoever praises the arbitrator — lo, this one curses the Omnipresent.
- L. "Concerning such a person it is said, 'He who blesses the arbitrator blasphemes the Lord (Ps. 10:3).'
- M. "But let justice pierce the mountain.
- N. "And so did Moses say, 'Let justice pierce the mountain.'"
- O. But Aaron would make peace between one person and another, as it is said, "He walked with me in peace and uprightness" (Mal. 2:6).

[1] Moses and Aaron actively participate in the formation of the law, and their dispute captures a Rabbinic engagement.

[2] The dispute is not a routine gloss.

[3] Moses is portrayed as a sage in the formation of the law.

[4] How is Moses comparable to sages in this document? Typical of the sages is engagement in disputes.

Tosefta Sanhedrin 4:7

A. "And he writes for himself a scroll of the Torah" (Deut. 17:17) —

L. R. Yosé says, "Ezra was worthy for the Torah to have been given by him, had not Moses come before him.

M. "Concerning Moses going up is stated, and concerning Ezra going up is stated.

N. "Concerning Moses going up is stated, as it is said, 'And Moses went up to God' (Ex. 19:3).

O. "And concerning Ezra going up is stated, as it is written, 'And he, Ezra, went up from Babylonia' (Ezra 7:6).

P. "Just as, in the case of going up mentioned in connection with Moses, he taught Torah to Israel, as it is stated, 'And the Lord commanded me at that time to teach you statutes and judgments' (Deut. 4:14),

Q. "so, in the case of going up mentioned in connection with Ezra, he taught Torah to Israel, as it is said, For 'Ezra had prepared his heart to expound the law of the Lord and to do it and to teach in Israel statutes and judgments' (Ezra 7:0)."

What marks Moses as a sage is his teaching of the Torah to Israel. Ezra illustrates the sage as model.

The Tosefta contains much more independent material than secondary and amplificatory expositions. Its narrative places Moses at the heart of virtue.

3

Moses in Sifra

I do not catalogue Leviticus' attributions to Moses of various declarations by God, thus "the Lord and to Moses saying…"

Sifra XCVIII:I

1. A. ["The Lord said to Moses, Take Aaron and Aaron and his sons did all the things which the Lord commanded by Moses" (Lev. 8:1-36).]
   B. "The Lord said to Moses, Take Aaron and his sons":
   C. Why does Scripture say this?
   D. Since it is said, "And the Lord sent a plague upon the people, because they made the calf which Aaron made" (Ex. 32:35),
   E. it is implied that Aaron had been rejected.
   F. Accordingly, when Scripture says, "The Lord said to Moses, Take Aaron and his sons," it is now implied that Aaron had been accepted once again.
2. A. How do we know that Moses realized that Aaron had been rejected?
   B. Since it is said, "And the Lord was so angry with Aaron that he was ready to destroy him; and I prayed for Aaron also at the same time" (Dt. 9:20), but Scripture does not go on to say, "and the Lord listened to me also that time."
   C. When, therefore, Scripture says, "The Lord said to Moses, Take Aaron and his sons," Moses knew that Aaron had been accepted once again.

Moses is routine, scarcely animate. He is skilled at interpreting God's messages. In Sifra he scarcely registers. Sifra does not set forth a proposition. The cogent indeed propositional exegesis of verses of Leviticus in the manner of Sifre to Numbers is absent. Sifra presents no proposition that concerns Moses.

4

Moses in Sifré to Numbers and Sifré Zutta to Numbers

The encounter with Scripture in Sifré to Numbers and Sifré Zutta to Numbers — as with Sifra — is comprised by the phrase, "And the Lord said to Moses, say to the people of Israel." I do not find many cases in Sifré to Numbers or in Sifré Zutta to Numbers in which Moses figures outside of the scriptural framework of serving as God's mouthpiece. Moses emerges as a sage equivalent to any other sage.

Sifré Zutta to Numbers VII.III:I.1.2.

A. "six covered wagons [and twelve oxen, a wagon for every two of the leaders, and for each one an ox, they offered them before the tabernacle. Then the Lord said to Moses, 'Accept these from them, that they may be used in doing the service of the tent of meeting, and give them to the Levites, to each man according to his service.' So Moses took the wagons and the oxen and gave them to the Levites]" (Num. 7:1-6):

B. "covered" means only, "shaded," as it is said, "and in litters and upon mules" (Is. 66:20).

C. R. Simeon says, "'covered' means only sealed, as it is said, 'And they shall bring your sons in their bosom' (Is. 49:22)."

D. R. Ishmael says, "'covered' means only, 'covered with drawings.'"

E. R. Nehemiah says, "'In the color of the firmament.'"

Naso VII.III:I.1.3.

A. "a wagon for every two of the leaders, and for each one an ox:"

B. How come they did not present half in oxen and half in wagons?

C. Moses was afraid that the ox of one of them might die, or that the wagon of one of them might be smashed, and it would turn out that that particular tribe might not have a share in the tabernacle.

D. And how do we know that the Omnipresent gave him the good news that none of the oxen would die and none of the wagons would be smashed? Say: "that they may be used in doing the service of the tent of meeting."

[1] Is Moses an active player or a routine and scarcely animate one? Moses figures as a conventional figure.

[2] What components of the collection make routine glosses of the received Scriptures and which ones provide more than minor glosses of the tradition? All the representations of Moses gloss the received Scripture, none breaks fresh ground.

[3] Entries that clarify Scripture are scattered without pattern in the Rabbinic canon.

[4] How is Moses comparable to sages in this document? Moses figures as a sage pure and simple.

BEHA'ALOTEKHA XII:I:I.1.

A. "Miriam and Aaron spoke against Moses (Num. 12:1-16):

B. "Miriam and Aaron spoke against Moses:" [The penalty for] wicked gossip is harsh, for Miriam was afflicted with the skin ailment only on account of wicked gossip, as it is said, "Miriam and Aaron spoke against Moses."

C. Miriam opened the subject and spoke to Aaron, and Aaron added to the matter of which she spoke and got involved in the subject.

D. R. Simeon says, "Also Zipporah opened the subject and spoke to Miriam, and Miriam added to the matter and spoke to Aaron, and Aaron added to the matter and got involved in the subject."

E. And what was the matter that he contributed?

F. They say: when the elders were appointed, all Israel kindled lights and made a celebration because seventy elders had ascended to authority. When Miriam saw these lights, she said, "Happy are these and happy are their wives!"

G. Said to her Zipporah, "Don't say 'and happy are their wives' but 'woe unto their wives.' For from the moment that the Holy One, blessed be he, spoke with your brother Moses, he has not laid a hand on me."

H. Immediately Miriam went to Aaron and they got involved in give and take over the matter. So it is said, "Miriam and Aaron spoke against Moses [because of the Cushite woman whom he had married]" — on the matter of his separation from the woman.

I. They said, "Moses was haughty. For did the Holy One blessed be he speak only with Moses? He had already spoken with many prophets and with us and we did not separate from our waves as he

4. Moses in Sifré to Numbers and Sifré Zutta to Numbers

has separated from his wife," as it is said, "Did the Lord speak only with Moses?"

Scripture is amplified but invokes no fresh perspectives.

PINHAS XXVII:XV:I.I.1

A. And Moses spoke to the Lord saying, ["Let the Lord, the God of the spirits of all flesh, appoint a man over the congregation, who shall go out before them an come in before them, who shall lead them out and bring them in; that the congregation of the Lord may not be as sheep which have no shepherd."
B. In the entire Torah this is the only place where the language appears, "And Moses spoke to the Lord saying."
C. He said to him, "Tell me if you are going to appoint someone else in my place."
D. And this is one of the things that Moses said before the Omnipresent: "Tell me if you act for me or if you do not act for me."
E. Said to him the Omnipresent, "I do act for you."
F. "And Moses spoke to the Lord saying" (Ex. 6:2): what does Scripture mean by "saying"?
G. He said to him, "Tell me if you are going to redeem them or if you are not going to redeem them."
H. Along these same lines you say: "And Moses cried out to the Lord saying, 'What shall I do with this people? In a little while they will stone me" (Ex. 17:4).
I. What is the meaning of "saying"?
J. He said "Tell me if I am going to fall by their hand or am not going to fall by their hand."
K. Along these same lines you say: "And Moses cried out to the Lord saying, 'God please heal her' (Num. 12:13),"
L. What is the meaning of "saying"?
M. He said to him, "Tell me if you are going to heal Miriam or of you are not going to heal Miriam."
N. Along these same lines you say: "And I beseeched the Lord at that time saying" (Dt. 3:23).
O. What is the meaning of "saying"?
P. He said to him, "Tell me lf I am going to enter the Land or if I am not going to enter the land."
Q. And here what does he say?
R. "And Moses spoke to the Lord saying."
S. What is the meaning of "saying"?
T. He said to him, "Tell me if you are going to appoint someone else in my place or if you are not going to appoint [someone else in my place."

The exposition amplifies the narrative of Moses but does not alter the sense of the received text.

[1] Is Moses an active player or a routine and scarcely animate one? Moses is no different from Scripture's portrait.

[2] Scriptures provide no more than minor glosses of the tradition.

[3] Entries that clarify Scripture through the contrast with tradition are scattered without pattern in the Rabbinic canon.

[4] How is Moses comparable to sages in this document? Moses is a standard sage. He is undistinguished.

5

Moses in Sifré to Deuteronomy

Sifré to Deuteronomy transforms cases into exemplary, general rules.

XIV:I

1. A. "You answered me and said, 'What you propose to do is good'" (Dt. 1:14-18):
   B. "What you should have said was, 'Our lord, Moses, from whom is it really fitting to study the Torah? From you or from your disciple or from your disciple's disciple? Is it not fitting to study the Torah from you, for you have suffered anguish on its account?'"
   C. That is in line with the facts in the following verses: "And he was there with the Lord forty days and forty nights" (Ex. 34:28).
   D. "And I stayed on the mountain forty days" (Dt. 9:9).
   E. [Moses continues,] "But I know that your real intention was this: 'Now he is going to appoint for us nearly eighty-thousand judges. If I am not one of them, my son will be, and if not my son, then my grandson. And we shall bring 'gifts' to such judges, and they will show us favor in court.'"
   F. That is why it is said, "You answered me and said, 'What you propose to do is good.'"
   G. [Moses continues,] "When I was slow about the matter, you said to me, 'Do it quickly.'"

[1] Is Moses an active player or a routine and scarcely animate one? Moses clarifies the sense of Scripture. But he has direct communication with God.

[2] Minor glosses of the tradition define Moses' role.

[3] Can we identify a pronounced bias? No.

[4] Moses is comparable to any sage.

XXVII:III

1. A. "...to show your servant the first works of your greatness":
   B. There are [1] those who called themselves servants, and the Holy One, blessed be He, called them servants, and [2] there are those who called themselves servants, and the Holy One, blessed be He, did not call them servants, and [3] there are those who did not call themselves servants, but the Holy One, blessed be He, called them servants:
[1] C. Abraham called himself a servant: "Do not pass away, I ask, from your servant" (Gen. 18:3), and the Holy One, blessed be He, called him a servant: "For my servant Abrahams sake" (Gen. 26:24).
   D. Jacob called himself a servant: "I am not worthy of all the mercies, and of all the truth, which you have shown to your servant" (Gen. 32:11), and God called him a servant: "But you, Israel, my servant" Is. 41:8).
   E. Moses called himself a servant: "To show your servant...," and the Holy One, blessed be He, also called him a servant: "My servant, Moses, is not so" (Num. 12:7).
   F. David called himself a servant: "I am your servant, the son of your servant-girl" (Ps. 116:16), and the Holy One, blessed be He, also called him a servant: "For I will defend this city to save it for my own sake and for the sake of my servant, David" (12 Kgs. 19:34), "And David my servant shall be their prince for ever" (Ez. 37:25).
   G. Isaiah called himself a servant: "And now says the Lord who formed me from the womb to be his servant" (Is. 49:5), and the Holy One, blessed be He, also called him a servant: "Like my servant Isaiah has walked naked and barefoot" (Is. 20:3).
[2] H. Samuel called himself a servant: "Then Samuel said, 'Speak, for your servant is listening'" (1 Sam. 3:10), but the Holy One, blessed be He, did not call him a servant.
   I. Samson called himself a servant: "You have given this great deliverance by the hand of your servant" (Judges. 115:18), but the Holy One, blessed be He, did not call him servant.
   J. Solomon called himself a servant: "Give your servant, therefore, an understanding heart" (1 Kgs. 3:9), but the Holy One, blessed be He, did not call him servant, but rather made him depend upon his father. David: "For David my servant's sake" (1 Kgs. 11:13).
[3] K. Job did not call himself a servant, but the Holy One, blessed be He, called him a servant: "You have considered my servant Job?" (Job 2:3).

5. Moses in Sifré to Deuteronomy

L. Joshua did not call himself a servant, but the Holy One, blessed be He, called him a servant: "Joshua the son of Nun, the servant of the Lord, died" (Josh. 24:29).

M. Caleb did not call himself a servant, but the Holy One, blessed be He, called him a servant: "But my servant, Caleb" (Num. 14:24).

N. Eliakim did not call himself a servant, but the Holy One, blessed be He, called him a servant: "That I will call my servant Eliakim" (Is. 22:20).

O. Zerubbabel did not call himself a servant, but the Holy One, blessed be He, called him a servant: "In that day, says the Lord of hosts, will I take you, O Zerubbabel, my servant, son of Shealtiel, and I will make you as a signet, for I have chosen you, says the Lord of hosts" (Hag. 2:23).

P. Daniel did not call himself a servant, but the Holy One, blessed be He, called him a servant: "O Daniel, servant of the living God" (Dan. 6:21).

Q. Hananiah, Mishael, and Azariah did not call themselves servants, but the Holy One, blessed be He, called them servants: "Shadrach, Meshach, and Abed-nego, you servants of God Most High, come forth and come here" (Dan. 3:26).

R. The former prophets did not call themselves servants, but the Holy One, blessed be He, called them servants: "For the Lord God will do nothing unless he tells his plan to his servants the prophets" (Amos 3:7).

Moses figures on a long catalogue of prophets and their distinguishing traits. All the members of the list exhibit traits in common. Moses is not a prophet among sages but the established pattern governs.

[1] Moses repeats a pattern.

[2] What components of the collection make routine glosses of the received Scriptures? A fixed pattern governs all the holy men.

[3] Can we identify a pronounced bias? The same virtue governs throughout.

[4] How is Moses comparable to sages in this document? All the sages follow a single pattern.

Moses is one among many iterations of a single pattern. They did not call themselves virtuous but God called them virtuous and so throughout, so Moses was the modest among many —all modest.

CCCV:I

1. A. "The Lord said to Moses, 'Take for yourself Joshua, son of Nun'" (Num. 27:18):

B. "Take for yourself": – a hero like yourself.

C. The Holy One, blessed be He, responded to Moses, saying to Moses, "Supply to Joshua a public loud-speaker, and let him present questions, expound the law, give out instructions, in your lifetime, so that when you leave this world, the Israelites should not say to him, 'During the lifetime of your master, you did not say a word, and now are you going to say a word?'"

2. A. And some say that [Moses] raised him off the ground and set him between his knees, so that Moses and the Israelites had to raise their heads to listen to the teachings of Joshua.
B. What did he say?
C. "Blessed is the Lord, who has given the Torah to Israel through our lord, Moses."
D. These were the words of Joshua.

3. A. R. Nathan says, "Moses was distressed in his heart that one of his sons did not stand forth [as leader]. Said to him the Holy One, blessed be He, 'Why are you distressed in your heart? Is it that one of your sons has not stood forth?
B. "'Now are not the sons of your brother, Aaron, tantamount to your own sons.
C. "'And so too the man whom I am setting up over Israel will go and stand at the door of Eleazar [the priest, Aaron's son].'
D. "To what may this be compared? To a mortal king who had a son who was not worthy of the throne. He took the throne from him and gave it to the son of his ally.
E. "He said to him, 'Even though I have assigned greatness to you, go and stand at my son's door.'
F. "So said the Holy One, blessed be He, 'Even though I have assigned greatness to you, go and stand at the door of Eleazar.'
G. "That is in line with this verse of Scripture: 'And he will stand before Eleazar the priest' (Num. 27:21).
H. "At that moment Moses's strength returned, and he encouraged Joshua before the presence of all Israel, as it is said, 'And then Moses called Joshua and said to him in the sight of all Israel, 'Be strong and resolute, [for it is you who shall go with this people in the land that the Lord swore to their fathers to give them, and it is you who shall apportion it to them. And the Lord himself will go before you. He will be with you. He will not fail you or forsake you. Fear not and be not dismayed]' (Dt. 31:7-8).
I. "He said to him, 'I hand this people over to you. They are still lambs. They are still children. Do not go nitpicking for every little thing that they do. For even their Lord did not go nitpicking for every little thing that they do.'
J. "And so Scripture says, 'When Israel was a child, then I loved him' (Hos. 11:1)."

5. Moses in Sifré to Deuteronomy

K. R. Nehemiah says, "'I do not have the right, but [if] I had the right, I should bring them in "beside shepherds' tents" (Song 1:8), to dwell therein.'"

Moses is every bit a human being, wanting too provide a high position to his sons. Joshua is the selected successor.
[1] Moses is an active player.
[2] The narrative provides more than minor glosses of the tradition.
[3] No pattern governs.
[4] We cannot classify the figure of Moses but impose a singular narrative.

CCCV:III

1. A. In a single year three righteous persons, Moses, Aaron, and Miriam died.
   B. The Israelites never again found solace after Moses, as it is said, "And I cut off the three shepherds in one month" (Zech. 11:8).
   C. But was it in one month [as Zechariah says,] and not in one year that they died?
   D. For it is said, "The great of the peoples are gathered together, the retinue of Abraham's God; [for the guardians of the earth belong to God; he is greatly exalted]" (Ps. 47:10).
   E. But when Miriam died, the well dried up, but then it returned on account of the merit of Moses and Aaron.
   F. When Aaron died, the pillar of cloud disappeared, but then both of them were restored through the merit of Moses.
   G. When Moses died, all three of them disappeared and did not come back.
2. A. At that time the Israelites were scattered and bereft of the merit of all religious duties. All the Israelites gathered to Moses and said to him, "Where is your brother, Aaron?"
   B. He said to them, "God has put him away in a secret place, for the life of the world to come."
   C. But they did not believe him. They said to him, "We know of you that you are merciless. Perhaps he said something to you that was not appropriate, and you imposed upon him the penalty of death!"
   D. What did the Holy One, blessed be He, do at that time? He brought the bier of Aaron and held it up in the heavens of heavens, and the Holy One, blessed be He, stood in lamentation over him, and the ministering angels responded to him.
   E. What did they say [in response to God's lamentation]? "The Torah of truth was in his mouth, and unrighteousness was not found in his lips; he walked with me in peace and uprightness and did turn many away from iniquity" (Ma. 2:6).

3. A. At that moment the Holy One, blessed be He, said to the angel of death, "Go, bring me the soul of Moses."
B. He went and stood before him and said to him, "Moses, give me your soul."
C. He said to him, "In a place in which I am in session, you have no right to stand, and yet you say to me, 'Give me your soul'? He growled at him and the other went forth in a huff.
D. The angel of death went and brought the tale back to the Omnipotent. Once again the Holy One, blessed be He, said to the angel of death, "Go, bring me the soul of Moses."
E. He went to where he was and looked for him but did not find him.
F. He went to the sea and said to it, "As to Moses, have you seen him?"
G. The sea said to him, "From the day on which he brought Israel through my midst, I have not seen him."
H. He went to the mountains and said to them, "As to Moses, have you seen him?"
I. They said to him, "From the day on which the Israelites received the Torah on Mount Sinai, we have not seen him."
J. He went to Gehenna and said to it, "As to Moses, have you seen him?"
K. It said to him, "I have heard his name, but him I have never seen."
L. He went to the ministering angels and said to them, "As to Moses, have you seen him?"
M. They said to him, "Go to mortals."
N. He went to Israel and said to them, "As to Moses, have you seen him?"
O. They said to him, "God knows his way. God has hidden him away for the life of the world to come, and no creature knows where he is."
P. For it is said, "And he was buried in the valley" (Dt. 34:6).
4. A. When Moses died, Joshua wept, crying out and mourning for him bitterly.
B. He said, "My father, my father, my lord, my lord.
C. "My father, for he raised me, my lord, for he taught me Torah."
D. And he mourned for him for many days, until the Holy One, blessed be He, said to Joshua, "Joshua, how long are you going to continue this mourning of yours? And has Moses died only unto you alone? And has he not died, also, unto me?
E. "For from the moment that he died, there has been deep mourning before me, as it is said, 'And in that day did the Lord, God of hosts, call to weeping and to lamentation' (Is. 22:12).
F. "But it is certain for him that he gains the world to come, as it is said, 'And the Lord said to Moses, Behold, you are going to sleep with your fathers and...will arise' (Dt. 31:16)."

5. Moses in Sifré to Deuteronomy

CCCXXXIX:I

1. A. "You shall die on the mountain that you are about to ascend [and shall be gathered to your kin, as your brother Aaron died on Mount Hor and was gathered to his kin]":
   B. He said before him, "Lord of the world, Why should I die? Is it not better for people to say, 'Moses is good,' because of what they have personally seen, than that they should say, 'Moses is good,' based on what they have heard? Is it not better that people should say, 'This is that very same Moses, who brought us out of Egypt, split the sea for us, brought down the manna for us, did wonders and acts of might for us,' than that they should say, 'Such and so is what Moses was, such and so is what Moses did'?"
   C. He said to him, "Go your way, Moses, it is a decree of mine that applies to every mortal."
   D. For it is said, "This is the Torah that applies to a mortal: when a person will die in a tent" (Num. 19:14).
   E. And further, "This is the Torah of a mortal, O Lord God" (2 Sam. 7:19).
2. A. The ministering angels said before the Holy One, blessed be He, "Lord of the world, why did the first man die?"
   B. He said to them, "Because he did not carry out my orders."
   C. They said to him, "Lo, Moses did carry out your orders."
   D. He said to them, "It is a decree of mine that applies to every mortal."
   D. For it is said, "This is the Torah that applies to a mortal: when a person dies in a tent" (Num. 19:14).

[1] Moses is a unique figure, with a number of patterned virtues, and he enjoys special merit in God's sight.

[2] The death narrative of Moses exhibits a number of special traits.

[3] Can we identify a pronounced bias or a polemical program in the unfolding entries that transform Moses the prophet and king of Israel into Rabbi Moses? Moses is a unique and saintly person.

[4] How is Moses comparable to sages in this document? Moses is different from the average sage, with traits to that mark him off.

CCCXLII:IV

1. A. "...the man of God":
   B. He was one of ten who were called "a man of God."
   C. Moses was called a man of God: "A prayer of Moses, the man of God" (Ps. 90:1).
   D. Elkanah: "And there came a man of God to Eli" (1 Sam. 2:27).
   E. Samuel: "Behold now, there is in this city a man of God" (1 Sam. 9:6).

F. David: "According to the commandment of David the man of God" (Neh. 12:24).
G. Shemaiah: "But the word of God came to Shemaiah the man of God saying" (1 Kgs. 12:22).
H. Iddo: "And behold there came a man of God out of Judah by the word of the Lord" (1 Kgs. 13:1).
I. Elijah: "O man of God, I pray you, let me life be precious" (2 Kgs. 1:13).
J. Elisha: "Behold now, I perceive that this is a holy man of God" (2 Kgs. 4:9).
L. Micah: "And a man of God came near and spoke to the king of Israel" (1 Kgs. 20:28).
M. Amoz: "But there came a man of God to him, saying, 'O king, let not the army of Israel go with you'" (2 Chr. 25:7).

Moses is one among ten who received the word of God and is not distinguished from the other nine prophets.

[1] Moses is routine and scarcely animate.

[2] Moses shares traits with other figures.

[3] Can we identify a pronounced bias or a polemical program in the unfolding entries that transform Moses the prophet and king of Israel into Rabbi Moses? The issue is not Moses the sage but Moses the prophet.

[4] How is Moses comparable to sages in this document? How else may we classify the figure of Moses if not as a sage in this document? Moses exemplifies the prophet.

6

Moses in Mekhilta Attributed to R. Ishmael

In its exegesis of Exodus Mekhilta Attributed to R. Ishmael sets forth a systematic account of Moses career.

XXIII:I.7.
A. "Then Moses stretched out his hand over the sea:"
B. The sea began to resist him.
C. Moses said to the sea in the name of the Holy One, blessed be he, to divide up, but it did not accept that order.
D. He showed it the staff, but it did not accept that order.
E. To what may the matter be compared? To the case of a king who had two gardens, one inside the other. He sold the inner one. The purchaser came to enter the inner garden, but the watchman would not let him in.
F. The purchaser said to the watchman in the name of the king, but he did not agree. He showed him the king's signet, and he did not agree. Finally the purchaser brought the king himself and he came. When the king came along, the watchman started to flee.
G. The purchaser said to him, "All day long I kept speaking to you in the name of the king, but you did not agree, and now how come you're running away?"
H. He said to him, "I'm not running away from you, but from the king."
I. So the Holy One, blessed be he, appeared in all his power and glory, the sea started to back off: "The sea saw him and fled" (Ps. 114:3).
M. Said Moses to the sea, "All day long I was telling you in the name of the Holy One, blessed be he, to divide up, but you did not accept that order.

N. "Now how come you are running away? 'What ails you, O see, that you flee' (Ps. 114:5)?"

O. The sea replied, "It is not on your account, Moses, it is not on your account, Son of Amram, but: 'Tremble, you earth, at the presence of the Lord, at the presence of the God of Jacob, who turned the rock into a pool of water, the flint into a fountain of waters' (Ps. 114:7-8)."

[1] Is Moses an active player or a routine and scarcely animate one? Moses is an active and important figure, commanding nature.

[2] What components of the collection make routine glosses of the received Scriptures and which ones provide more than minor glosses of the tradition? There is nothing minor in Moses' position in this narrative, which places Moses in command of the ocean.

[3] Can we identify a pronounced bias or a polemical program in the unfolding entries that transform Moses the prophet and king of Israel into Rabbi Moses? Or are the entries that clarify Scripture through the contrast with tradition scattered without pattern in the Rabbinic canon? Moses is a wonderworker and outshines rabbis on the course of the narrative.

[4] How is Moses comparable to sages in this document? How else may we classify the figure of Moses if not as a sage in this document? Here Moses is not a standard rabbi, a sage.

XLI:II.10.

A. [As the Lord commanded Moses, so Aaron placed it before the testimony to be kept.] And the people of Israel ate the manna forty years:"

B. R. Joshua says, "For forty days after the death of Moses the Israelites ate manna.

C. "How so? On the seventh of Adar Moses died. They ate manna therefore for the twenty-four days of Adar that were left, as well as for sixteen days of Nisan.

D. "For it is said, 'And the manna ceased on the morrow, after they had eaten of the produce of the land' (Josh. 5:12); 'And they ate of the produce of the land on the morrow after the passover, unleavened cakes and parched corn' (Josh. 5:11)."

E. R. Eleazar the Modiite says, "For seventy days after the death of Moses the Israelites at manna.

F. "How so? On the seventh of Adar Moses died. They ate manna therefore for the twenty-four days of Adar that were left, as well as the thirty days of the second Adar — that year having been intercalated with an extra month — as well as for sixteen days of Nisan.

G. "For it is said, 'And the manna ceased on the morrow, after they had eaten of the produce of the land' (Josh. 5:12); 'And they ate of

6. Moses in Mekhilta Attributed to R. Ishmael

the produce of the land on the morrow after the passover, unleavened cakes and parched corn' (Josh. 5:11).''

H. R. Eliezer says, "For seventy days after the death of Moses the Israelites ate manna.

I. "How so? On the seventh of Shebat Moses died. They ate manna therefore for the twenty-four days of Shebat that were left, as well as the thirty days of Adar — that year not having been intercalated with an extra month — as well as for sixteen days of Nisan.

J. "For it is said, 'And the manna ceased on the morrow, after they had eaten of the produce of the land' (Josh. 5:12); 'And they ate of the produce of the land on the morrow after the passover, unleavened cakes and parched corn' (Josh. 5:11)."

K. R. Yosé says, "For fifty-four years the Israelites ate the manna, forty while Moses was alive, fourteen after he died.

L. "For Scripture says, 'And the people of Israel ate the manna forty years, till they came to a habitable land; they ate the manna, till they came to the border of the land of Canaan.'

M. "For why should Scripture say, 'till they came to the border of the land of Canaan'? But this refers to the fourteen years that the Israelites at the manna after the death of Moses,

N. "the seven years during which they conquered the land, and the seven years during which they divided it up."

11. A. When Miriam died, the well dried up.
B. When Aaron died, the pillar of cloud disappeared.
C. When Moses died, the manna was taken away.
D. R. Joshua says, "When Miriam died, the well dried up, but then it returned on account of the merit of Moses and Aaron.
E. "When Aaron died, the pillar of cloud disappeared, but then both of them were restored through the merit of Moses.
F. "When Moses died, all three of them — the well, the pillar of cloud, and the manna — disappeared and did not come back.
G. "And the hornet did not cross the Jordan along with them."

The death of Moses, Miriam and Aaron marked a number of events of consequence. Moses implicitly represented a holy man, But he doe not engage in holy actions on his own part. Moses is not a holy man, he is an instrument of God. The next pericope makes this position explicit.

XLIII:III.1.

A. "Whenever Moses held up his hand, [Israel prevailed; and whenever he lowered his hand, Amalek prevailed]:"

B. Now is it really so that the hands of Moses made the Israelites win or the hands of Moses broke Amalek?

C. But all the time that Moses raised up his hands to the heaven, the Israelites looked to him and believed in the One who had commanded Moses to do it that way, and the Omnipresent then did wonders and acts of might for them.

2. A. Along these same lines: "The Lord said to Moses, 'Make yourself a fiery serpent'" (Num. 21:8):
   B. Now could the snake kill or bring to life?
   C. But all the time that Moses did so, the Israelites looked to him and believed in the One who had commanded Moses to do it that way, and the Omnipresent then sent healing to them.
3. A. Along these same lines: "And the blood shall be to you as a token" (Ex. 12:13):
   B. Now what value did the blood have for the angel or for the Israelites for that matter?
   C. But all the time that the Israelites did so, putting blood on their doors, the Holy One, blessed be he, had mercy on them:
   D. The Lord will pass over" (Ex. 12:23).
4. A. R. Eliezer says, "What is the point of the statement, 'Whenever Moses held up his hand, Israel prevailed,' and what is the point of the statement, 'and whenever he lowered his hand, Amalek prevailed'?
   B. "So long as Moses raised his hands upward, the Israelites were destined to be strengthened through teachings of the Torah which were going to be given through his hands.
   C. "So long as Moses lowered his hands, the Israelites were destined to lower themselves from words of the Torah which were going to be given through his hands."
5. A. "But Moses' hands grew weary:"
   B. In this connection [we learn that] one should not postpone doing religious duties.
   C. For had Moses not said to Joshua, "Choose men for us," he would not have been distressed in this way.
6. A. They said that at that moment the hands of Moses were heavy.
   B. It was like a man who had two jugs of water hanging from his hands.
7. A. "so they took a stone and put it under him [and he sat upon it]:"
   B. Didn't they have some sort of pillow or cushion or bolster to put under Moses?
   C. But Moses said...[this alludes to a pericope that is not cited here].
8. A. "and Aaron and Hur held up his hands, [one on one side, and the other on the other side]:"
   B. For he would raise and lower them.
9. A. "so his hands were steady until the going down of the sun:"
   B. "This indicates that they were observing a fast [to sunset]," the words of R. Joshua.
   C. R. Eleazar the Modiite says, "Sin at that moment weighed heavily on Moses's hands. He could not withstand it. What did he do? He turned to the deeds of the patriarchs:
   D. "'so they took a stone and put it under him:' this refers to the deeds of the patriarchs.
   E. "'and he sat upon it:' this refers to the deeds of the matriarchs."

6. Moses in Mekhilta Attributed to R. Ishmael

10. A. "and Aaron and Hur held up his hands, [one on one side, and the other on the other side]:"
    B. Why does Scripture say, "one on one side, and the other on the other side"?
    C. It is because Aaron would call to mind the deeds of Judah, and Hur would call to mind the deeds of Levi.
    D. In this connection sages say, "They have no fewer than three persons passing before the ark on the day of a public fast."
11. A. "so his hands were steady:"
    B. With one hand [he called attention to the fact that] he had not received a thing from the Israelites.
    C. And with the other hand Moses said before the Holy One, blessed be he, "Lord of the world! Through my hands you brought the Israelites out of Egypt, through my hands you split the Red Sea for them, through my hands you did wonder and acts of might for them, and so too, through my hands you should now do wonders and acts of might for them."
12. A. "[so his hands were steady] until the going down of the sun:"
    B. Since we have learned in connection with all the other kingdoms that they make war only to the sixth hour of the day.
    C. But as to this culpable kingdom, it made war from dawn to dusk.
13. A. "And Joshua mowed down Amalek and his people [with the edge of the sword]:"
    B. R. Joshua says, "He went down and chopped off the heads of the heroes who were with him standing at the head of the battle lines."
    C. R. Eleazar the Modiite says, "[The word for 'mowed down'] serves as an acronym: he made them sick, he made them tremble, he crushed them."
14. A. "Amalek:"
    B. This means Amalek literally.
    C. The use of the accusative particle serves to encompass his wife and children.
    D. "his people:"
    E. this refers to his troops who were with him.
    F. And when the word "and" is added, it serves to encompass the troops with his sons.
15. A. "with the edge of the sword:"
    B. R. Joshua says, "He did not disfigure them but judged them with mercy."
16. A. R. Eliezer says, "'with the edge of the sword:' why is this said?
    B. "We learned that this war was carried out only at the instruction of the Almighty."
17. A. Others say, "This verse of Scripture was carried out in their regard:
    B. "'Therefore as I live, says the Lord God, I will prepare you for blood, and blood shall pursue you; surely you have hated your own blood, therefore blood shall pursue you' (Ez. 35:6)."

This elaborate exposition stresses the secular character of Moses and other holy people. This is stated explicitly: Now is it really so that the hands of Moses made the Israelites win or the hands of Moses broke Amalek? But all the time that Moses raised up his hands to the heaven, the Israelites looked to him and believed in the One who had commanded Moses to do it that way

XLIV:I.3.

A. "and recite it in the ears of Joshua:"
B. "This indicates that on that day Joshua was anointed," the words of R. Joshua.
C. R. Eleazar the Modiite says, "This is one of four righteous men to whom a hint [of what was coming] was given. Two of them perceived, and two of them did not perceive it.
D. "To Moses a hint was given, but he did not perceive it.
E. "To Jacob a hint was given, but he did not perceive it.
F. "To David and Mordecai hints were given, and they perceived them."

4. A. How do we know the case of Moses? It is said, "and recite it in the ears of Joshua.'" He so said to him, "Joshua will bring about Israel's inheritance of the land." But in the end, Moses stood and pleaded: "And I besought the Lord" (Dt. 3:23).
B. To what may the matter be likened? To the case of a king who made a decree concerning his son that he not come into his palace with him. He entered the first gate, but people kept silence, the second, but people kept silence, the third, and people rebuked him, saying to him, "It is enough for you! To this point!"
C. So too when Moses had conquered the territory of the two peoples, the land of Sihon and Og, and gave it to the tribe of Reuben and of Gad and the half-tribe of Manasseh, they said to him, "It appears that the decree has been made only conditionally. So too, we have been judged only conditionally."
D. Said Moses before the Holy One, blessed be he, "Lord of the age, perhaps your way is like the way of a mortal. If an administrator makes a decree, a prefect can force its revocation. If a prefect makes a decree, a commander can force its revocation. If a commander makes a decree, a general can force its revocation. When a general makes a decree, a governor can force him to revoke it. When a governor makes a decree, a viceroy can make him revoke it. When a viceroy makes a decree, the principal ruler can make him revoke it. For all of them are appointed, one above the next in succession: 'For one higher than the high watches' (Qoh 5:7).
E. "'Are your ways like their ways?'"

10. A. "But the Lord was angry with me on your account:"
B. R. Eleazar b. R. Simeon says, "[Moses said,] 'With me he spoke in a harsh way,' which is not possible for a mortal to say.

6. Moses in Mekhilta Attributed to R. Ishmael

    C.   "[Moses continues,] 'Perhaps you might suppose that it was on my account?' Scripture is explicit: 'on your account,' meaning, 'on your account, not on my account.'

    D.   "'You are the ones who caused me not to enter the land of Israel.'"

11. A.   "And the Lord said to me, 'It is enough for you'" (Dt. 3:24):

    B.   He said to him, "It is enough for you! To this point!"

12. A.   ["And the Lord said to me, 'It is enough for you'" (Dt. 3:24):]

    B.   R. Joshua says, "'It is enough for you:' It is enough for you to have the world to come."

13. A.   Now Moses was yet standing and pleading, setting forth all those pleas.

    B.   Said Moses before him, "Lord of the world, was a decree made that I personally shall not enter the land?

    C.   "'Therefore you shall not bring this assembly' (Num. 20:12): as ruler I shall not enter, let me enter as a commoner."

    D.   He said to him, "A king may never thereafter enter as a commoner."

    E.   Now Moses was yet standing and pleading, setting forth all those pleas.

    F.   Said Moses before him, "Lord of the world, since a decree has been made that I shall not enter the land either as king or as commoner, let me enter it by the cave of Caesarion below Paneas."

    G.   He said to him, "But you shall not go over there" (Dt. 34:4).

    H.   He said before him, "Lord of the world, since a decree has been issued that I shall not enter the land either as king or as commoner, not even by the cave of Caesarion below Paneas, then at least let my bones cross the Jordan."

    I.   He said to him, "But you shall not go over this Jordan" (Dt. 3:27).

14. A.   R. Simeon b. Yohai says, "It is hardly necessary to demonstrate matters in this way. Is it not in fact said: 'But I must die in this land, I must not go over the Jordan' (Dt. 4:22)?

    B.   "How is it possible for a corpse to cross?

    C.   "Rather, they said to Moses, 'Even your bones are not going to cross the Jordan.'"

15. A.   R. Hananiah b. Iddi says, "Moses was weeping for himself:

    B.   "'But I must die in this land, I must not go over the Jordan' (Dt. 4:22).

    C.   "'For you are to pass over the Jordan' (Dt. 11:31).

    D.   "'You are going to cross the Jordan but I am not going to.'"

16. A.   Others say, "Moses was bending over the feet of Eleazar, saying to him, 'Eleazar, son of my brother, seek mercy for me as I sought mercy for your father, Aaron.'

    B.   "'Moreover the Lord was very angry with Aaron to have destroyed him, but I prayed for Aaron also' (Dt. 9:20)."

17. A.   He said before him, "Lord of the world, if so, let me at least see it from a distance."

    B.   And as to that matter, he said to him, "Go up to the top of Pisgah" (Dt. 3:27).

18. A. R. Hananiah b. Aqabia says, "The view given to Abraham our father was more accommodating than the view accorded to Moses.
    B. "For as to Abraham, he was not put to any trouble, while Moses was put to trouble.
    C. "In the case of Abraham: 'Lift up your eyes and look from the place where you are located, northward, southward, eastward, and westward' (Gen. 13:15).
    D. "In the case of Moses: 'Go up to the top of Pisgah and lift up your eyes westward, northward, southward, and eastward, and look with your eyes' (Dt. 3:27).
    E. "'Go up there, look around, and only then will you see.'"
19. A. How do we know that whatever Moses asked to see, the Holy One, blessed be he, showed him?
    B. "And the Lord showed him all the land" (Dt. 34:1), that is, the land of Israel.
    C. He wanted to see the house of the sanctuary, and he showed it to him: "Even Gilead" (Dt. 34:1), which only means the Temple, "Gilead, you are to me the head of Lebanon" (Jer. 22:6).
    D. How do we know that he showed him Samson, son of Manoah? "As far as Dan" (Dt. 34:1); 'And there was a man of Zorah, of the family of Dan, whose name was Manoah" (Judges 13:2).
20. A. Another interpretation of the phrase, "As far as Dan" (Dt. 34:1):
    B. The tribes had not yet entered the land, and the land of Israel had not yet been divided among the Israelites, so how can Scripture say, "As far as Dan" (Dt. 34:1)?
    C. He had earlier said to Abraham, "Twelve tribes are destined to come forth from your loins, and this is the portion of one of them."
21. A. Along these same lines: "And pursued as far as Dan" (Gen. 14:14):
    B. The tribes had not yet entered the land, and the land of Israel had not yet been divided among the Israelites, so how can Scripture say, "And pursued as far as Dan" (Gen. 14:14)?
    C. The Holy One, blessed be he, said to our father, Abraham, "In this place your descendants are destined to worship an idol."
    D. Abraham's strength then failed him.

Moses argues with God. He contends on a fundamental issue. He does not argue as a sage with another counterpart-sage.

[1] Is Moses an active player or a routine and scarcely animate one? Moses in the end must be seen as active, drawing upon the heritage of Scripture.

[2] What components of the collection make routine glosses of the received Scriptures and which ones provide more than minor glosses of the tradition? Moses's role in the exposition is powerful.

[3] Can we identify a pronounced bias or a polemical program in the unfolding entries that transform Moses the prophet and king of Israel into Rabbi Moses? Moses is an active player in the dispute with God, and his argument is elaborate.

[4] How is Moses comparable to sages in this document? Moses is like a sage, arguing independent of God.

7

Moses in Genesis Rabbah

Genesis Rabbah sets forth highly propositional statements on Creation. It makes the same point many times and registers a coherent account of the book of Genesis

VIII:VIII.1.

A. R. Samuel bar Nahman in the name of R. Jonathan: "When Moses was writing out the Torah, he wrote up the work of each day [in sequence]. When he came to the verse, 'And God said, "Let us make man...,' (Gen. 1:26), he said, 'Lord of the age, in saying this you give an opening to heretics [to claim that there are two dominions in heaven, so the creator-God had to consult with others in making the world, because he was not alone and all-powerful].'

B. "He said to him, 'Write it anyhow, and if someone wants to err, let him err.'

C. "The Holy One, blessed be he, said to him, 'Moses, as to this man whom I am going to create, will I not bring forth both great and unimportant descendants from him?

D. "It is so that, if a great man has to get permission from a lesser person and says, 'Why in the world should I have to get permission from an unimportant person,' people will say to him, 'Learn a lesson from your creator, who created the creatures of the upper world and the creatures of the lower world, but when he came to create man, went and took counsel with the ministering angels.'"

Moses engages in a discussion with God and has no important independent stance. God's is the principal voice,

XXX:VIII.

1. A. c):

B. Bar Hotah said, "Whoever is described as 'blameless' lived out his years to the full limit of a septennate. [He lived a multiple of seven years after this epithet was applied to him. Thus Noah lived 350 years after the Flood.]"

2. A. R. Yohanan said, "Whoever is described with the verb to be, [as in 'Noah was...,'] remained just as he was, beginning to end."

B. The following objection was raised: "And lo, it is written, 'Abraham was one, and he inherited the earth' (Ez. 33:24). On the basis of the use of the word 'one' do we know that he was one, beginning to end? [Surely he changed in the course of his life.]"

C. He said to him, "Indeed, this item does not contradict my proposition." [We shall now carry forward this statement.]

D. R. Yohanan and R. Hanina both said, "At the age of forty-eight, Abraham came to recognize his creator. Then how in his regard can one understand the use of the word 'was,' [since he was not the same, beginning and end, but vastly changed in his life]? He was designated to lead the entire world to repentance."

E. [Continuing the former proposition:] "The use of the word 'was' in the case of 'Man was...,' (Gen. 3:22) means that the first man was designated for death.

F. "The use of the word 'was' in the case of the snake (Gen. 3:1) means that the snake was designated as the vehicle of punishment.

G. "The use of the word 'was' in the case of Cain (Gen. 4:2) means that Cain was designated to go into exile.

H. "The use of the word 'was' in the case of Job ["Job was...," (Job 1:1)] means that Job was designated for suffering.

I. "The use of the word 'was' in the case of Noah means that Noah was designated for the performance of a miracle.

J. "The use of the word 'was' in the case of Moses [at Ex. 3:1] means that Moses was designated to serve as the redeemer.

K. "The use of the word 'was' in the case of Mordecai [Est. 2:5] means that he was designated for redemption."

Moses takes up a position in a list of exegeses of a biblical usage.

XXXI:VIII.

1. A. "Make yourself an ark" (Gen. 6:14):

B. Said R. Issi, "In four passages a statement is made in this manner: 'Make yourself....' In three of those passages, the matter [of how to do so] is fully spelled out, but in one of them it is not spelled out.

C. "'Make yourself an ark — of gopher wood' (Gen. 6:14)."

D. (R. Nathan said, "With beams of cedar.")

E. [Continuing Issi's exposition:] "'Make yourself knives — of flint' (Josh. 5:2), which is explained as flint knives.

7. Moses in Genesis Rabbah

F. "'Make yourself two trumpets — of silver' (Num. 10:2), so the matter is explicitly clarified.

G. "But as to the statement, 'Make yourself a fiery snake' (Num. 21:5), that is not spelled out [for the material to be used is not specified."

H. [The reason is that Moses could figure it out for himself, as we shall now see.] R. Yudan in the name of R. Assi: "'The wise man may hear and increase in learning' (Prov. 1:6) refers to Moses.

I. "He said, 'If I make it of gold or of silver, the sounds of the language will not correspond to one another, [since the Hebrew word for snake, *nahash,* and the words for silver and gold, *kesef, zahav,* do not sound the same.] Lo, I shall make it out of copper, for the sound of the word for copper, *nehoshet,* sounds the same as the word for snake, *nahash,* hence 'a copper snake' (Num. 21:9)."

J. On the basis of this passage you may draw the conclusion that the Torah was given in the Holy Language [Hebrew].

K. R. Phineas and R. Hilqiah in the name of R. Simon: "Just as the Torah was given in the Holy Language, so the world was created in the Holy Language.

L. "Have you ever heard someone say, *gini, ginia, itha, ittha, antropi, antropia, gabra, gabretha*? [*Gini* and *antropi* are woman and man in Greek, *ittha* and *gabra* are the same for Aramaic. These words lack the corresponding feminine or masculine forms, such as are seen in *ish* and *ishshah*]."

M. "Why then are the Hebrew forms *ish* and *ishshah*? Because the forms correspond to one another [which proves that Hebrew is older than the other languages]."

Moses on his own could figure out the rules under which he was governed,

LXV:I.

1. A. "When Esau was forty years old, he took to wife Judith, the daughter of Beeri, the Hittite, and Basemath the daughter of Elon the Hittite; and they made life bitter for Isaac and Rebecca" (Gen. 26:34-35):

B. "The swine out of the wood ravages it, that which moves in the field feeds on it" (Ps. 80:14).

C. R. Phineas and R. Hilqiah in the name of R. Simon: "Among all of the prophets, only two of them spelled out in public [the true character of Rome, represented by the swine], Asaf and Moses.

D. "Asaf: 'The swine out of the wood ravages it.'

E. "Moses: 'And the swine, because he parts the hoof' (Deut. 14:8).

F. "Why does Moses compare Rome to the swine? Just as the swine, when it crouches, puts forth its hoofs as if to say, 'I am clean,' so the wicked kingdom steals and grabs, while pretending to be setting up courts of justice.

G. "So Esau, for all forty years, hunted married women, ravished them, and when he reached the age of forty, he presented himself to his father, saying, 'Just as father got married at the age of forty, so I shall marry a wife at the age of forty.'

H. "'When Esau was forty years old, he took to wife Judith, the daughter of Beeri, the Hittite, and Basemath the daughter of Elon the Hittite.'"

Moses explains the rule governing the swine.

C:X.1.

A. "So Joseph dwelt in Egypt, he and his father's house, and Joseph lived a hundred and ten years" (Gen. 50:22):
B. There were six paired heroes who lived the same period of time, Rebecca and Kohath, Levi and Amram, Joseph and Joshua, Samuel and Solomon, Moses and Hillel the Elder, and R. Yohanan ben Zakkai and R. Aqiba.
C. Moses lived forty years in Pharaoh's palace, then forty years in Midian, and served Israel for forty years.
D. Hillel the Elder came up from Babylonia at the age of forty, served as disciple of sages forty years, and served Israel for forty years.
E. R. Yohanan b. Zakkai was in business for forty years, studied the Torah for forty years, and served Israel for forty years.
F. R. Aqiba spent forty years in ignorance, studied for forty years, and served Israel for forty years.

Moses is an example of a rule, not an important actor.

XCVII:III.3.

D. An example of this is that wherever R. Yosé the tall appeared, Rabbi also made an appearance.
E. "'Am I now come [for the first time]?' [Certainly not.] I was with Moses, your master, but he prayed and said, 'If your presence does not go with me, do not carry us up from here' (Ex. 33:15). [Moses did not want the angel to come, so he did not come, but now he has made his appearance.] I could not go back upward to heaven, because I had not then carried out my assignment, but I could not go down below, for he was still praying [against my coming], saying, 'If your presence does not go with me, do not carry us up from here.' So be careful not to do to me what your master Moses did, on account of which I was driven out."

[1] Is Moses an active player or a routine and scarcely animate one? Like the document before us, so too Moses' comments are random and do not yield a coherent pattern.

[2] What components of the collection make routine glosses of the received Scriptures and which ones provide more than minor glosses of the tradition? This is indicated at the relevant passage.

7. Moses in Genesis Rabbah

[3] Can we identify a pronounced bias or a polemical program in the unfolding entries that transform Moses the prophet and king of Israel into Rabbi Moses? Or are the entries that clarify Scripture through the contrast with tradition scattered without pattern in the Rabbinic canon? Moses is generally framed as a sage.

[4] How is Moses comparable to sages in this document? How else may we classify the figure of Moses if not as a sage in this document? Moses engages in discussions with God, but he is reckoned as a sage.

8

Moses in Leviticus Rabbah

The mixed character of Genesis Rabbah joins propositional to exegetical rhetoric. That is in order to make points of both general intelligibility and also very specific and concrete amplification of detail. Leviticus Rabbah marks a transitional moment in the workings of Midrash. Exactly what did the framers of Leviticus Rabbah learn when they opened the book of Leviticus? When they read the rules of sanctification of the priesthood, they heard the message of the salvation of all Israel. Leviticus became the story of how Israel, purified from social sin and sanctified, would be saved.

XIII:V. 1.

A. Said R. Ishmael b. R. Nehemiah, "All the prophets foresaw what the pagan kingdoms would do [to Israel].

9. A. Moses foresaw what the evil kingdoms would do [to Israel].

B. "The camel, rock badger, and hare" (Deut. 14:7). [Compare: "Nevertheless, among those that chew the cud or part the hoof, you shall not eat these: the camel, because it chews the cud but does not part the hoof, is unclean to you. The rock badger, because it chews the cud but does not part the hoof, is unclean to you. And the hare, because it chews the cud but does not part the hoof, is unclean to you, and the pig, because it parts the hoof and is cloven-footed, but does not chew the cud, is unclean to you" (Lev. 11:4-8).]

C. The camel (GML) refers to Babylonia, [in line with the following verse of Scripture: "O daughter of Babylonia, you who are to be devastated!] Happy will be he who requites (GML) you, with what you have done to us" (Ps. 147:8).

D. "The rock badger" (Deut. 14:7) — this refers to Media.

> E. Rabbis and R. Judah b. R. Simon.
> F. Rabbis say, "Just as the rock badger exhibits traits of uncleanness and traits of cleanness, so the kingdom of Media produced both a righteous man and a wicked one."
> G. Said R. Judah b. R. Simon, "The last Darius was Esther's son. He was clean on his mother's side and unclean on his father's side."
> H. "The hare" (Deut 14:7) — this refers to Greece. The mother of King Ptolemy was named "Hare" [in Greek: <u>lagos</u>].
> I. "The pig" (Deut. 14:7) — this refers to Edom [Rome].
> J. Moses made mention of the first three in a single verse and the final one in a verse by itself (Deut. 14:7, 8). Why so?
> K. R. Yohanan and R. Simeon b. Laqish.
> L. R. Yohanan said, "It is because [the pig] is equivalent to the other three."
> M. And R. Simeon b. Laqish said, "It is because it outweighs them."
> N. R. Yohanan objected to R. Simeon b. Laqish, "'Prophesy, therefore, son of man, clap your hands [and let the sword come down twice, yea thrice]'" (Ez. 21:14).
> O. And how does R. Simeon b. Laqish interpret the same passage? He notes that [the threefold sword] is doubled (Ez. 21:14).

This is characteristic of the presentation of Moses as a prophet like all other prophets. He is not only declared to be like the prophets but he is shown to talk like a prophet and to say what prophets say. Moses is captured as a principal voice in Israel: Moses foresaw what the evil kingdoms would do [to Israel].

[1] Is Moses an active player or a routine and scarcely animate one? Moses follows a strict pattern that applies to other prophets.

[2] What components of the collection make routine glosses of the received Scriptures and which ones provide more than minor glosses of the tradition? Moses's adherence to the received pattern marks him as a copycat.

[3] Can we identify a pronounced bias or a polemical program in the unfolding entries that transform Moses the prophet and king of Israel into Rabbi Moses? Or are the entries that clarify Scripture through the contrast with tradition scattered without pattern in the Rabbinic canon? There is no bias particular to the exposition of Moses's position.

[4] How is Moses comparable to sages in this document? Moses is pronouncedly comparable to a prophet sharing the disciplines of the other named prophets.

> 10. A. (Gen. R. 65:1:) R. Phineas and R. Hilqiah in the name of R. Simon: "Among all the prophets, only two of them revealed [the true evil of Rome], Assaf and Moses.
> B. "Assaf said, 'The pig out of the wood ravages it' (Ps. 80:14).
> C. "Moses said, 'And the pig, [because it parts the hoof and is cloven-footed but does not chew the cud]' [Lev. 11:7].

8. Moses in Leviticus Rabbah

D. "Why is [Rome] compared to a pig?
E. "It is to teach you the following: Just as, when a pig crouches and produces its hooves, it is as if to say, 'See how I am clean [since I have a cloven hoof],' so this evil kingdom acts arrogantly, seizes by violence, and steals, and then gives the appearance of establishing a tribunal for justice."

Moses is classified as a prophet.

4. A. R. Joshua of Sikhnin in the name of R. Levi: "Moses did not feast his eyes on the Presence of God, but he benefited from the Presence.
B. "How do we know that he did not feast his eyes on the Presence of God? 'And Moses hid his face' [Ex. 3:6].
C. "And how do we know that he benefited from the Presence? 'And Moses did not know that a beam of light shown from his face' [Ex. 34:29].
D. "As a reward for the fact that 'Moses hid his face,' he had the merit [stated in the following verse]: 'And the Lord spoke to Moses face to face' [Ex. 33:11].
E. "As a reward for the fact that 'He was afraid' [Ex. 3:6], he had the merit [stated in the following verse]: 'And the people were afraid to come near him' [Ex. 34:30].
F. "As a reward for his refraining from 'looking upon' [the face of God] [Ex. 3:6], he had the merit [stated in the following verse]: 'And he will look upon the likeness of the Lord' [Num. 12:8].
G. "Nadab and Abihu, for their part, did feast their eyes upon the Presence of God, but then they did not benefit from the Presence of God."

[1] Is Moses an active player or a routine and scarcely animate one? Moses is an active and virtuous figure.

[2] What components of the collection make routine glosses of the received Scriptures and which ones provide more than minor glosses of the tradition? This is a well articulated proposition about Moses the prophet.

[3] Can we identify a pronounced bias or a polemical program in the unfolding entries that transform Moses the prophet and king of Israel into Rabbi Moses? The polemic contrasts Moses and the sons of Aaron,

[4] How is Moses comparable to sages in this document? He is exemplary and subject to divine favor.

9

Moses in Pesiqta Derab Kahana

A compilation of twenty-eight propositional discourses, some of them borrowed from the base-document, Pesiqta deRab Kahana innovates because it appeals for its themes and lections to the liturgical calendar, rather than to a Pentateuchal book.

II:X.6.A. R. Judah bar Simon in the name of R. Yohanan: "There were three statements that Moses heard from the mouth of the Almighty, on account of which he was astounded and recoiled.
B. "When he said to him, And they shall make me a sanctuary [and I shall dwell among them] (Ex. 25:8), said Moses before the Holy One, blessed be He, 'Lord of the ages, lo, the heavens and the heavens above the heavens cannot hold you, and yet you yourself have said, And they shall make me a sanctuary [and I shall dwell among them].'
C. "Said to him the Holy One, blessed be He, 'Moses, it is not the way you are thinking. But there will be twenty boards' breadth at the north, twenty at the south, eight at the west, and I shall descend and shrink my Presence among you below.'
D. "That is in line with this verse of Scripture: And I shall meet you there (Ex. 25:20).
E. "When he said to him, My food which is presented to me for offerings made by fire [you shall observe to offer to me] (Num. 28:2), said Moses before the Holy One, blessed be He, 'Lord of the ages, if I collect all of the wild beasts in the world, will they produce one offering [that would be adequate as a meal for you]?

F. "'If I collect all the wood in the world, will it prove sufficient for one offering,' as it is said, Lebanon is not enough for altar fire, nor the beasts thereof sufficient for burnt-offerings (Is. 40:16).

G. "Said to him the Holy One, blessed be He, "Moses, it is not the way you are thinking. But: You shall say to them, This is the offering made by fire [he lambs of the first year without blemish, two day by day] (Num. 28:3), and not two at a time but one in the morning and one at dusk, as it is said, One lamb you will prepare in the morning, and the other you will prepare at dusk (Num. 28:4).'

H. "And when he said to him, When you give the contribution to the Lord to make expiation for your lives (Ex. 30:15), said Moses before the Holy One, blessed be He, 'Lord of the ages, who can give redemption-money for his soul?

I. "'One brother cannot redeem another (Ps. 49:8), for too costly is the redemption of men's souls (Ps. 49:9).'

J. "Said the Holy One, blessed be He, to Moses, 'It is not the way you are thinking. But: This they shall give — something like this [namely, the half-shekel coin] they shall give.'"

7. A. R. Huna in the name of Rab, "Almighty — we cannot find him out, great one in strength (Job 37:23): we have not yet found out the strength of the Holy One, blessed be He, for the Holy One, blessed be He, does not impose burdens on Israel. [He accepts only a half-shekel.]

B. "And when Moses heard this, he began to praise Israel, saying, Happy is the people whose God is the Lord, happy is the people for whom such is the case (Ps. 144:15). Happy is the one whose help is the God of Jacob (Ps. 146:5)."

No. 6 provides a composite of three cases in which God's requirements are shown to be moderate indeed, scarcely commensurate to God's glory, and No. 7 then goes over the same matter.

[1] Is Moses an active player or a routine and scarcely animate one? He lays out the question which God answers.

[2] What components of the collection make routine glosses of the received Scriptures and which ones provide more than minor glosses of the tradition? These are not minor glosses but principal statements of fundamental propositions.

[3] Can we identify a pronounced bias or a polemical program in the unfolding entries that transform Moses the prophet and king of Israel into Rabbi Moses? Yes, there is a clear program in operation.

[4] How is Moses comparable to sages in this document? Hs raises questions of a rational order.

V:VI 1. A. *Hark! My beloved! Here he comes, bounding over the mountains, leaping over the hills:"*

C. R. Judah says, *"Hark! My beloved! Here he comes* refers to Moses.

9. Moses in Pesiqta Derab Kahana

D. "When Moses came and said to Israel, 'In this month you will be redeemed,' they said to him, 'Moses, our lord, how are we going to be redeemed? Did not the Holy One, blessed be He, say to our father, Abraham, *"your descendants will be sojourners in a land that is not theirs and they will be slaves there, and they will be oppressed for four hundred years"* (Gen. 15:13)? And is it not the case that we have to our account only two hundred and ten years [of slavery in Egypt]?'

E. "He said to them, 'Since he wants to redeem you, he does not pay attention to your accounts. But *bounding over the mountains, leaping over the hills* means that he is skipping over foreordained calculations of the end and over all reckonings and times.

F. "'In this month you will be redeemed: *This month is for you the beginning of months* (Ex. 12:2).'"

Moses explains God's program. [1] Is Moses an active player or a routine and scarcely animate one? Moses is a principal player in God's program.

[2] What components of the collection make routine glosses of the received Scriptures and which ones provide more than minor glosses of the tradition? This is more than a minor gloss. It is a direct challenge to Moses's authority.

[3] Can we identify a pronounced bias or a polemical program? There is a polemic throughout that sets forth a reasonable and rational program of Scripture interpretation.

[4] How is Moses comparable to sages in this document? Moses is a sage advocating a reasonable program of interpretation of Scripture.

["*Hark! My beloved! Here he comes* refers to Moses.]

B. "When Moses came and said to Israel, 'In this month you will be redeemed,' they said to him, 'Moses, our lord, how are we going to be redeemed? And the land of Egypt is filled with the filth of idolatry that belongs to us.'

C. "He said to them, 'Since he wants to redeem you, he does not pay attention to your idolatry. But he goes *bounding over the mountains, leaping over the hills,* and hills refers to idolatry, in line with this verse: *On the tops of mountains they make sacrifices and in hills they offer incense* (Hos. 4:12).'"

God is once more the subject of rational exposition. Moses clarifies God's instructions.

3. A. Rabbis say, "*Hark! My beloved! Here he comes* refers to Moses.

B. "When Moses came and said to Israel, 'In this month you will be redeemed,' they said to him, 'Moses, our lord, how are we going to be redeemed? And we have no good deeds to our credit.'

C. "He said to them, 'Since he wants to redeem you, he does not pay attention to your wicked deeds. But to whom does he pay attention?

To the righteous who are among you, for example, Amram and his court.

D. "For *hills and mountains* refers only to courts, in line with this verse: *That I may go and seek out upon the mountains* (Judges 11:37)."

The same judgment applies.

4. A. R. Judah bar Simon in the name of R. Yohanan: "There were three statements that Moses heard from the mouth of the Almighty, on account of which he was astounded and recoiled.

B. "When he said to him, *And they shall make me a sanctuary [and I shall dwell among them]* (Ex. 25:8), said Moses before the Holy One, blessed be He, 'Lord of the age, lo, the heavens and the heavens above the heavens cannot hold you, and yet you yourself have said, *And they shall make me a sanctuary [and I shall dwell among them]* .'

C. "Said to him the Holy One, blessed be He, 'Moses, it is not the way you are thinking. But there will be twenty boards' breadth at the north, twenty at the south, eight at the west, and I shall descend and shrink my Presence among you below.'

D. "That is in line with this verse of Scripture: *And I shall meet you there* (Ex. 25:20).

E. "When he said to him, *My food which is presented to me for offerings made by fire [you shall observe to offer to me]* (Num. 28:2), said Moses before the Holy One, blessed be He, 'Lord of the age, if I collect all of the wild beasts in the world, will they produce one offering [that would be adequate as a meal for you]?

F. "'If I collect all the wood in the world, will it prove sufficient for one offering,' as it is said, *Lebanon is not enough for altar fire, nor the beasts thereof sufficient for burnt-offerings* (Is. 40:16).

G. "Said to him the Holy One, blessed be He, "Moses, it is not the way you are thinking. But: *You shall say to them, This is the offering made by fire [the lambs of the first year without blemish, two day by day]* (Num. 28:3), and not two at a time but one in the morning and one at dusk, as it is said, *One lamb you will prepare in the morning, and the other you will prepare at dusk* (Num. 28:4).'

H. "And when he said to him, *When you give the contribution to the Lord to make expiation for your lives* (Ex. 30:15), said Moses before the Holy One, blessed be He, 'Lord of the age, who can give redemption-money for his soul?

I. "'*One brother cannot redeem another* (Ps. 49:8), *for too costly is the redemption of men's souls* (Ps. 49:9).'

J. "Said the Holy One, blessed be He, to Moses, 'It is not the way you are thinking. But: *This they shall give* – something like this [namely, the half-shekel coin] they shall give"

9. Moses in Pesiqta Derab Kahana

The daily whole-offering effects atonement for sins of the preceding day. Moses is a rational figure,. not a prophetic one.

1. A. *And Moses took the bones of Joseph with him* (Ex. 13:19):
   B. This tells you how praiseworthy was Moses.
   C. For all the Israelites were occupied in despoiling Egypt, while Moses was occupied with the bones of Joseph.
   D. That is in line with this verse of Scripture: *And Moses took the bones of Joseph with him* (Ex. 13:19).
   E. *With him,* said R. Yohanan, refers to *with him* in the camp.
2. A. Who told Moses were Joseph was born? They say as follows:
   B. Serah, daughter of Asher, was in that generation, and she told Moses, "Moses, it is in the River Nile that Joseph is buried."
   C. Moses went and stood at the bank of the Nile River and said, "Joseph, Joseph, the hour has come for the Holy One, blessed be He, to redeem his children.
   D. "The Presence of God is held up for you, the Israelites are held up for you, the clouds of glory are held up for you.
   E. "If you now show yourself, well and good, but if not, lo, we are free of the oath that you have imposed on us."
   F. At that moment the ark of Joseph floated upward to the surface.
   G. And some say that he took a shred and wrote the Ineffable Name of God on it, and tossed it into the water.
   H. At that moment the ark of Joseph floated upward to the surface.
3. A. There were two dogs, conjured by magicians, who began to bark at Moses. Moses said, "People, you will see [what these are]. Real dogs do not bark, fake dogs bark."
   B. Said R. Yudan, "It was because that dog snarled, while, *And to all the children of Israel a dog did not show its tongue* (Ex. 11:7) [that Moses knew these were fake dogs]."

Moses is a wonderworker.

[1] Moses is a distinctive figure and highly animate.

[2] What components of the collection make routine glosses of the received Scriptures and which ones provide more than minor glosses of the tradition? There is nothing routine in the portrait of Moses here.

[3] Can we identify a pronounced bias or a polemical program in the unfolding entries that transform Moses the prophet and king of Israel into Rabbi Moses? Moses is not a rabbi here, but a wonder worker. But he does invoke the authority of reason here.

10

Moses in Esther Rabbah I

6. A. When Moses was told, "And rehearse it in the ears of Joshua" (Ex. 17:14), it was an indication to him that he would die, and Joshua would lead the Israelites into the land.
   B. And yet: "And I besought the Lord" (Dt. 3:23).
   H. As to Moses: to begin with, he fled from Pharaoh, and now he drowned him in the sea. This proves that he saw a new age.
   I. As to Job: to begin with, Scripture says, "He pours out my gall upon the ground" (Job 16:13).
   J. And now, Scripture says of him, "And the Lord gave Job twice as much as he had before" (Job 42:10). This proves that he saw a new age.
   K. As to Mordecai: to begin with, "He put on sackcloth with ashes" (Est. 4:1). But now: "He went forth from the presence of the king in royal apparel" (Est. 8:15). [This proves that he saw a new age.]

Moses is no different from the other holy men.

11

Moses in Song of Songs Rabbah

Song of Songs is read by the sages as a paean of praise to Israel by God.

XX:1

6. A. R. Judah b. R. Simon made two statements:
   B. "Just as an apple costs only a penny, but you can smell its fragrance any number of times,
   C. "So said Moses to the Israelites, 'If you wish to be redeemed, you may be redeemed for a simple matter.'
   D. "They may be compared to someone who had sore feet and he went to all the physicians for healing and was not healed. Then he came to one, who said to him, 'If you want to be healed, you can be healed in a simple way. Plaster your feet with bullshit.'
   E. "So said Moses to the Israelites, 'If you wish to be redeemed, you may be redeemed for a simple matter.'
   F. "'"And you shall take a bunch of hyssop and dip it"' (Ex. 12:22).
   G. "They said to him, 'Our lord, Moses, how much does this bundle of hyssop cost? Four or five cents?'
   H. "He said to them, 'Even a penny. But it will make it possible for you to inherit the spoil of Egypt, the spoil at the Sea, the spoil of Sihon and Og, and the spoil of the thirty-one kings [of Canaan].'
   I. "The palm-branch [for the Festival of Tabernacles], which costs someone a good dollar, and through which one carries out a variety of religious duties, all the more so!
   J. "Therefore Moses admonishes Israel, 'And you shall take for yourself on the first day' (Lev. 23:40)."

[1] Moses is an active player and teaches healing to the Israelites.
[2] We have little more than minor glosses of the tradition.

[3] We identify a polemical program in favor of simplicity.

[4] How is Moses comparable to sages in this document? Sages demand simple gifts.

12

Moses in Ruth Rabbah

Like the other Midrash-compilations of its class, Ruth Rabbah makes one paramount point through numerous exegetical details. Along these same lines, Ruth Rabbah has only one message, expressed in a variety of components but single and cogent.

III:III

1. A. R. Nehemiah commenced discourse by citing the following verse: "'Your prophets have been like foxes among ruins, O Israel. You have not gone up into the breaches or built up a wall for the house of Israel, that it might stand in battle in the day of the Lord' (Ez. 13:4-5):
   B. "Just as a fox spies out in the ruins for a place to flee when it sees people coming, so 'Your prophets have been like foxes among ruins, O Israel. You have not gone up into the breaches,'
   C. "like Moses.
   D. "To whom may our lord Moses be compared?
   E. "To a faithful shepherd, whose fence collapsed at twilight.
   F. "He went and repaired it on three sides, but a breach remained on the fourth.
   G. "Since he had no time to repair it before dark; he himself stood in the breach.
   H. "Came a lion, and he stood against it.
   I. "Came a wolf, and he stood against it.
   J. "But as for you, 'You have not gone up into the breaches,' like Moses.
   K. "For had you thrust yourselves into the breach like Moses, you would have been able to stand in war on the day of the wrath of the Lord."

L. [Supply: "And it came to pass in the days when the judges ruled, there was a famine in the land."]

Moses stands up for Israel. [1] Moses is an active player. [2] He provides more than minor glosses of the tradition.

[3] We identify a pronounced bias that transform Moses the prophet and king of Israel into Rabbi Moses.

[4] Moses is courageous and stands up against Israel's enemies.

III:III 3.

A. R. Menahem b. Abin interpreted the verse to speak of Moses:

B. "'[The sons of Shelah son of Judah: Er father of Lecah, [Laadah father of Mareshah, and the families of the linen factory at Bethashbea;] and Jokim, [and the men of Cozeba and Joash, and Saraph, who married into Moab and Jashubi Lehem (the records are ancient). These are the potters who dwelt at Netaim and Gederah; they dwelt there in the king's service]' (1 Chr. 4:21-23).

C. "'...and Jokim': in line with the verse, 'Rise up, O Lord, and let your enemies be scattered' (Num. 10:35). [The word for 'rise up' uses the letters that serve Jokim.]

D. "'...and the men of Cozeba': for he belied the word of the Holy One, blessed be He: 'Lord, why do you lose your temple against your people' (Ex. 32:11).

E. "'...and Joash': since he despaired for his life: 'And if not, blot me, I pray you, out of your book which you have written' (Ex. 32:32).

F. '...and Saraph': for he called to mind the deed of those who were to be burned to death: 'Remember Abraham, Isaac, and Israel your servants' (Ex. 32:13).

G. "'...who married into Moab': whose pleasant deeds came and went up before his father in heaven.

H. "'...and Jashubi Lehem': who ascended on high and captured the Torah: 'You have ascended on high, you have led an exile into captivity' (Ps. 68:19). [The word for 'capture' and Jashubi use the same letters.]

I. "...the records are ancient":

M. [Supply: "the records are ancient":]

N. R. Judah b. R. Simon said, "These words are incomprehensible here but are spelled out in another passage: 'And the Lord said to Moses, write these words, after the manner of the words' (Ex. 34:27)."

O. "These are the potters": in line with this verse: "And the Lord formed man" (Gen. 2:7) [since the word for potter and form use the same consonants].

P. Another reading of "These are the potters": these are the souls of the righteous, with whom the Holy One, blessed be He, took counsel

12. Moses in Ruth Rabbah

R. "...who dwelt at Netaim and Gederah [plants and hedges]':

S. "plants': in line with this verse: "And the Lord God planted a garden" (Gen. 2:8).

T. "...and hedges": in line with the following verse: "who have placed the sand for the margin of the sea" (Jer. 5:22).

U. "...they dwelt there in the king's service": With the King of kings of kings, the Holy One, blessed be He, dwelt the souls of the righteous, with whom he took counsel in creating the world.

[1] Moses is a routine and scarcely animate one.

[2] The exegetes of Scripture make routine glosses.

[3] The entries that clarify Scripture are scattered without pattern in the Rabbinic canon

[4] Moses is not comparable to sages in this document.

XXI:1

10. A. Hadrian – may his bones rot! – asked R. Joshua b. Hananiah, saying to him, "I am better off than your lord, Moses."

B. He said to him, "Why?"

C. "Because I am alive and he is died, and it is written, 'For to him who is joined to all living there is hope; for a living dog is better than a dead lion' (Qoh. 9:4)."

D. He said to him, "Can you make a decree that no one kindle a fire for three days?"

E. He said to him, "Yes."

F. At evening the two of them went up to the roof of the palace. They saw smoke ascending from a distance.

G. He said to him, "What is this?"

H. He said to him, "It is a sick noble. The physician came to him and told he will be healed only if he drinks hot water."

I. He said to him, "May your spirit go forth [drop dead]! While you are still alive, your decree is null.

J. "But from the time that our lord, Moses, made the decree for us, 'You shall not burn a fire in your dwelling place on the Sabbath day' (Ex. 35:3), no Jew has ever kindled a flame on the Sabbath, and even to the present day, the decree has not been nullified.

K. "And you say you are better off than he is?"

Moses' decree is carried out.

13

Moses in Lamentations Rabbah

Lamentations Rabbah emphases that everything that happens to Israel makes sense and bears meaning; and Israel is not helpless before its fate but controls its own destiny. This is the one and whole message of our compilation, and it is the only message that is repeated throughout; everything else proves secondary and derivative of the fundamental proposition that the destruction of the Temple in Jerusalem in 70 C.E. — as much as in 586 B.C.E. — proves the enduring validity of the covenant, its rules and its promise of redemption. Moses takes a larger role in Lamentations Rabbah than in any other document.

XXIV.ii.

1. A. Another interpretation of the passage, "My Lord God of Hosts summoned on that day to weeping and lamenting tonsuring and girding with sackcloth:"
   B. When the Holy One, blessed be He, considered destroying the house of the sanctuary, he said, "So long as I am within it, the nations of the world cannot lay a hand on it.
   C. "I shall close my eyes to it and take an oath that I shall not become engaged with it until the time of the end."
   D. Then the enemies came and destroyed it.
   E. Forthwith the Holy One, blessed be He, took an oath by his right hand and put it behind him: "He has drawn back his right hand from before the enemy" (Lam. 2:3).
   F. At that moment the enemies entered the sanctuary and burned it up.
   G. When it had burned, the Holy One, blessed be He, said, "I do not have any dwelling on earth any more. I shall take up my presence from there and go up to my earlier dwelling."

H. That is in line with this verse: "I will go and return to my place, until they acknowledge their guilt and seek my face" (Hos. 5:15).

I. At that moment the Holy One, blessed be He, wept, saying, "Woe is me! What have I done! I have brought my Presence to dwell below on account of the Israelites, and now that they have sinned, I have gone back to my earlier dwelling. Heaven forefend that I now become a joke to the nations and a source of ridicule among people."

J. At that moment Metatron came, prostrated himself, and said before him, "Lord of the world, let me weep, but don't you weep!"

K. He said to him, "If you do not let me weep now, I shall retreat to a place in which you have no right to enter, and there I shall weep."

L. That is in line with this verse: "But if you will not hear it, my soul shall weep in secret for pride" (Jer. 13:17).

2. A. Said the Holy One, blessed be He, to the ministering angels, "Let's go and see what the enemies have done to my house."

B. Forthwith the Holy One, blessed be He, and the ministering angels went forth, with Jeremiah before them.

C. When the Holy One, blessed be He, saw the house of the sanctuary, he said, "This is certainly my house, and this is my resting place, and the enemies have come and done whatever they pleased with it!"

D. At that moment the Holy One, blessed be He, wept, saying "Woe is me for my house! O children of mine – where are you? O priests of mine – where are you? O you who love me – where are you? What shall I do for you? I warned you, but you did not repent."

E. Said the Holy One, blessed be He, to Jeremiah, "Today I am like a man who had an only son, who made a marriage canopy for him, and the son died under his marriage canopy. Should you not feel pain for me and for my son?

F. "Go and call Abraham, Isaac, Jacob, and Moses from their graves, for they know how to weep."

G. He said before him, "Lord of the world, I don't know where Moses is buried."

H. The Holy One, blessed be He, said to him, "Go and stand at the bank of the Jordan and raise your voice and call him, 'Son of Amram, son of Amram, rise up and see your flock, which the enemy has swallowed up!'"

I. Jeremiah immediately went to the cave of Machpelah and said to the founders of the world, "Arise, for the time has come for you to be called before the Holy One, blessed be He."

J. They said to him, "Why?"

K. He said to them, "I don't know," because he was afraid that they would say to him, "In your time this has come upon our children!"

L. Jeremiah left them and went to the bank of the Jordan and cried out, "Son of Amram, son of Amram, rise up, for the time has come for you to be called before the Holy One, blessed be He."

13. Moses in Lamentations Rabbah

M. He said to him, "What makes this day so special, that I am called before the Moses Holy One, blessed be He?"
N. He said to them, "I don't know."
O. He left him and went to the ministering angels, for he had known them from the time of the giving of the Torah. He said to them, "You who serve on high! Do you know on what account I am summoned before the Holy One, blessed be He?"
P. They said to him, "Son of Amram! Don't you know that the house of the sanctuary has been destroyed, and the Israelites taken away into exile?"
Q. So he cried and wept until he came to the fathers of the world. They too forthwith tore their garments and put their hands on their heads, crying and weeping, up to the gates of the house of the sanctuary.
R. When the Holy One, blessed be He, saw them, forthwith: "My Lord God of Hosts summoned on that day to weeping and lamenting, to tonsuring and girding with sackcloth."
S. Were it not stated explicitly in a verse of Scripture, it would not be possible to make this statement.
T. And they went weeping from this gate to that, like a man whose deceased lies before him,
U. and the Holy One, blessed be He, wept, lamenting, "Woe for a king who prospers in his youth and not in his old age."

3. A. Said R. Samuel bar Nahman, "When the Temple was destroyed, Abraham came before the Holy One, blessed be He, weeping, pulling at his beard and tearing his hair, striking his face, tearing his clothes, with ashes on his head, walking about the temple, weeping and crying, saying before the Holy One, blessed be He,
B. "'How come I am treated differently from every other nation and language, that I should be brought to such humiliation and shame!'
C. "When the ministering angels saw him, they too [Cohen, p. 43:] composed lamentations, arranging themselves in rows, saying,
D. "'the highways lie waste, the wayfaring man ceases' (Isa. 33:8)."
E. "What is the meaning of the statement, 'the highways lie waste'?
F. "Said the ministering angels before the Holy One, blessed be He, 'The highways that you paved to Jerusalem, so that the wayfarers would not cease, how have they become a desolation?'
G. "'the wayfaring man ceases:'
H. "Said the ministering angels before the Holy One, blessed be He, 'How have the ways become deserted, on which the Israelites would come and go for the pilgrim festivals?'
I. "'You have broken the covenant:'
J. "Said the ministering angels before the Holy One, blessed be He, 'Lord of the world, the covenant that was made with their father, Abraham, has been broken, the one through which the world was settled and through which you were made known in the world,

that you are the most high God, the one who possesses heaven and earth.'
K. "'He has despised the cities:'
L. "Said the ministering angels before the Holy One, blessed be He, 'You have despised Jerusalem and Zion after you have chosen them!
M. "Thus Scripture says, 'Have you utterly rejected Judah? Has your soul loathed Zion?' (Jer. 14:19).
N. "'He regards not Enosh:'
O. "Said the ministering angels before the Holy One, blessed be He, 'Even as much as the generation of Enosh, chief of all idol worshippers, you have not valued Israel!'
P. "At that moment the Holy One, blessed be He, responded to the ministering angels, saying to them, 'How come you composing lamentations, arranging themselves in rows, on this account?'
Q. "They said to him, 'Lord of the world! It is on account of Abraham, who loved you, who came to your house and lamented and wept. How come you didn't pay any attention to him?'
R. "He said to them, 'From the day on which my beloved died, going off to his eternal house, he has not come to my house, and now "what is my beloved doing in my house" (Jer. 11:15)?'
S. "Said Abraham before the Holy One, blessed be He, 'Lord of the world! How come you have sent my children into exile and handed them over to the nations? And they have killed them with all manner of disgusting forms of death! And you have destroyed the house of the sanctuary, the place on which I offered up my son Isaac as a burnt-offering before you!?'
T. "Said to Abraham the Holy One, blessed be He, 'Your children sinned and violated the whole Torah, transgressing the twenty-two letters that are used to write it: "Yes, all Israel have transgressed your Torah" (Dan. 9:11).'
U. "Said Abraham before the Holy One, blessed be He, 'Lord of the world, who will give testimony against the Israelites, that they have violated your Torah?'
V. "He said to him, 'Let the Torah come and give testimony against the Israelites.'
W. "Forthwith the Torah came to give testimony against them.
X. "Said Abraham to her, 'My daughter, have you come to give testimony against the Israelites that they have violated your religious duties? and are you not ashamed on my account? Remember the day on which the Holy One, blessed be He, peddled you to all the nations and languages of the world, and no one wanted to accept you, until my children came to Mount Sinai and they accepted you and honored you! And now are you coming to give testimony against them on their day of disaster?'
Y. "When the Torah heard this, she went off to one side and did not testify against them.

13. Moses in Lamentations Rabbah

Z. "Said the Holy One, blessed be He, to Abraham, 'Then let the twenty-two letters of the alphabet come and give testimony against the Israelites.'

AA. "Forthwith the twenty-two letters of the alphabet came to give testimony against them.

BB. "The aleph came to give testimony against the Israelites, that they had violated the Torah.

CC. "Said Abraham to her, 'Aleph, you are the head of all of the letters of the alphabet, and have you now come to give testimony against the Israelites on the day of their disaster?'

DD. "'Remember the day on which the Holy One, blessed be He, revealed himself on Mount Sinai and began his discourse with you: "I [*anokhi*, beginning with aleph] am the Lord your God who brought you out of the Land of Egypt, out of the house of bondage" (Ex. 20:2).

EE. "'But not a single nation or language was willing to take you on, except for my children! And are you now going to give testimony against my children?'

FF. "Forthwith the aleph went off to one side and did not testify against them.

GG. "The *bet* came to give testimony against the Israelites.

HH. "Said Abraham to her, 'My daughter, have you come to give testimony against my children, who are meticulous about the Five Books of the Torah, at the head of which you stand, as it is said, "In the beginning [*bereshit*] God created..." (Gen. 1:1)?'

II. "Forthwith the bet went off to one side and did not testify against them.

JJ. "The gimmel came to give testimony against the Israelites.

KK. "Said Abraham to her, 'Gimmel, have you come to give testimony against my children, that they have violated the Torah? Is there any nation, besides my children, that carries out the religious duty of wearing show-fringes, at the head of which you stand, as it is said, "Twisted cords [*gedelim*] you shall make for yourself" (Dt. 22:12).'

LL. "Forthwith the gimmel went off to one said and did not testify against them.

MM. "Now when all of the letters of the alphabet realized that Abraham had silenced them, they were ashamed and stood off and would not testify against Israel.

NN. "Abraham forthwith commenced speaking before the Holy One, blessed be He, saying to him, 'Lord of the world, when I was a hundred years old, you gave me a son. And when he had already reached the age of volition, a boy thirty-seven years of age, you told me, "offer him up as a burnt-offering before me"!

OO. "'And I turned mean to him and had no mercy for him, but I myself tied him up. Are you not going to remember this and have mercy on my children?'

PP. "Isaac forthwith commenced speaking before the Holy One, blessed be He, saying to him, 'Lord of the world, when father said to me, "God will see to the lamb for the offering for himself, my son" (Gen. 22:8), I did not object to what you had said, but I was bound willingly, with all my heart, on the altar, and spread forth my neck under the knife. Are you not going to remember this and have mercy on my children!'

QQ. "Jacob forthwith commenced speaking before the Holy One, blessed be He, saying to him, 'Lord of the world, did I not remain in the house of Laban for twenty years? And when I went forth from his house, the wicked Esau met me and wanted to kill my children, and I gave myself over to death in their behalf. Now my children are handed over to their enemies like sheep for slaughter, after I raised them like fledglings of chickens. I bore on their account the anguish of raising children, for through most of my life I was pained greatly on their account. And now are you not going to remember this and have mercy on my children?'

RR. "Moses forthwith commenced speaking before the Holy One, blessed be He, saying to him, 'Lord of the world, was I not a faithful shepherd for the Israelites for forty years? I ran before them in the desert like a horse. And when the time came for them to enter the land, you issued a decree against me in the wilderness that there my bones would fall. And now that they have gone into exile, you have sent to me to mourn and weep for them.'

SS. "This is in line with the proverb people say: 'When it's good for my master, it's not good for me, but when its bad for him, it's bad for me!'

TT. "Then Moses said to Jeremiah, 'Go before me, so I may go and bring them in and see who will lay a hand on them.'

UU. "Said to him Jeremiah, 'It isn't even possible to go along the road, because of the corpses.'

VV. "He said to him, 'Nonetheless.'

WW. "Forthwith Moses went along, with Jeremiah leading the way, until they came to the waters of Babylon.

XX. "They saw Moses and said to one another, 'Here comes the son of Amram from his grave to redeem us from the hand of our oppressors.'

YY. "An echo went forth and said, 'It is a decree from before me.'

ZZ. "Then said Moses to them, 'My children, to bring you back is not possible, for the decree has already been issued. But the Omnipresent will bring you back quickly.' Then he left them.

AAA. "Then they raised up their voices in weeping until the sound rose on high: 'By the rivers of Babylon there we sat down, yes, we wept' (Ps. 137:1).

BBB. "When Moses got back to the fathers of the world, they said to him, 'What have the enemies done to our children?'

13. Moses in Lamentations Rabbah

CCC. "He said to them, 'Some of them he killed, the hands of some of them he bound behind their back, some of them he put in iron chains, some of them he stripped naked, some of them died on the way, and their corpses were left for the vultures of heaven and the hyenas of the earth, some of them were left for the sun, starving and thirsting.'

DDD. "Then they began to weep and sing dirges: 'Woe for what has happened to our children! How have you become orphans without a father! How have you had to sleep in the hot sun during the summer without clothes and covers! How have you had to walk over rocks and stones without shoes and sandals! How were you burdened with heavy bundle of sand! How were your hands bound behind your backs! How were you left unable even to swallow the spit in your mouths!'

EEE. "Moses then said, 'Cursed are you, O sun! Why did you not grow dark when the enemy went into the house of the sanctuary?'

FFF. "The sun answered him, 'By your life, Moses, faithful shepherd! They would not let me nor did they leave me alone, but beat me with sixty whips of fire, saying, "Go, pour out your light."'

GGG "Moses then said, 'Woe for your brilliance, O temple, how has it become darkened? Woe that its time has come to be destroyed, for the building to be reduced to ruins, for the school children to be killed, for their parents to go into captivity and exile and the sword!'

HHH. "Moses then said, 'O you who have taken the captives! I impose an oath on you by your lives! If you kill, do not kill with a cruel form of death, do not exterminate them utterly, do not kill a son before his father, a daughter before her mother, for the time will come for the Lord of heaven to exact a full reckoning from you!'

III. "The wicked Chaldeans did not do things this way, but they brought a son before his mother and said to the father, 'Go, kill him!' The mother wept, her tears flowing over him, and the father hung his head.

JJJ. "And further Moses said before him, 'Lord of the world! You have written in your Torah, "Whether it is a cow or a ewe, you shall not kill it and its young both in one day" (Lev. 22:28).

KKK. "'But have they not killed any number of children along with their mothers, and yet you remain silent!'

LLL. "Then Rachel, our mother, leapt to the fray and said to the Holy One, blessed be He, 'Lord of the world! It is perfectly self-evident to you that your servant, Jacob, loved me with a mighty love, and worked for me for father for seven years, but when those seven years were fulfilled, and the time came for my wedding to my husband, father planned to substitute my sister for me in the marriage to my husband. Now that matter was very hard for me, for I knew the deceit, and I told my husband and gave him a sign by which he would know the difference between me and my sister, so that my father would not be able to trade me off. But then I regretted it and I bore my passion, and I had mercy for my sister, that she should not be shamed. So in the evening for my husband they substituted my sister for me, and I gave my sister all the signs that I had given to my husband, so that he would think that she was Rachel.

MMM. "'And not only so, but I crawled under the bed on which he was lying with my sister, while she remained silent, and I made all the replies so that he would not discern the voice of my sister.

NNN. "'I paid my sister only kindness, and I was not jealous of her, and I did not allow her to be shamed, and I am a mere mortal, dust and ashes. Now I had no envy of my rival, and I did not place her at risk for shame and humiliation. But you are the King, living and enduring and merciful. How come then you are jealous of idolatry, which is nothing, and so have sent my children into exile, allowed them to be killed by the sword, permitted the enemy to do whatever they wanted to them?!'

OOO. "Forthwith the mercy of the Holy One, blessed be He, welled up, and he said, 'For Rachel I am going to bring the Israelites back to their land.'

PPP. "That is in line with this verse of Scripture: 'Thus said the Lord: A cry is heard in Ramah, wailing, bitter weeping, Rachel weeping for her children. She refuses to be comforted for her children, who are gone. Thus said the Lord, Restrain your voice from weeping, your eyes from shedding tears; for there is a reward for your labor, declares the Lord; they shall return from the enemy's land, and there is hope for your future, declares the Lord: your children shall return to their country'" (Jer. 31:15-17)."

XXXV.I.

1. A. "How lonely sits the city:"
   B. Three prophets made use of the word "how" in stating their prophecies, and these are they: Moses, Isaiah, and Jeremiah.
   C. Moses said, "How can I myself alone bear your burden" (Dt. 1:12).
   D. Isaiah said, "How is the faithful city become a harlot" (Isa. 1:21).
   E. Jeremiah said, "How lonely sits the city."
2. A. Said R. Levi, "The matter may be compared to the case of a noble lady who had three representatives of her family at hand. One of them saw her when she was prosperity, one saw her when she was confused, one of them saw her when she was degraded.
   B. "So Moses saw Israel in their prosperity: 'How can I myself bear up under the weight of your prosperity?' (Deut. 1:12).
   C. "Isaiah saw them in their confusion and said, 'Alas, she has become a harlot' (Isaiah 1:21).
   D. "Jeremiah saw them in their utter degradation and said, 'How [lonely sits the city that was full of people! How like a widow has she become, she that was great among the nations! She that was a princess among the cities has become a vassal. She weeps bitterly

13. Moses in Lamentations Rabbah

        in the night, tears on her cheeks, among all her lovers she has none to comfort her; all her friends have dealt treacherously with her, they have become her enemies]' (Lamentations 1:1-2).

E.   "'How lonely sits the city....'"

[1] Is Moses an active player or a routine and scarcely animate one? Moses plays a critical role in the narrative.

[2] Moses is not a routine figure but an original and important one.

[3] The entries that clarify Scripture treat Moses as original and important, equivalent to Abraham Isaac and Jacob,

[4] How is Moses comparable to sages in this document? How else may we classify the figure of Moses if not as a sage in this document? And we must treat Moses as equivalent to patriarchs, and he is the only biblical figure redrawn as patriarch.

14

Moses in the Fathers According to Rabbi Nathan

In ARNA Moses is the subject of an elaborate and systematic exposition. The collection of stories about Rabbi Moses is the largest of any tractate's. In 250 C. E. Mishnah-tractate Abot, The Fathers, delivered its message through aphorisms assigned to named sages. A few centuries later — the date is indeterminate but it is possibly ca. 500 — the Fathers According to Rabbi Nathan, a vast secondary expansion of that same tractate, endowed those anonymous names with flesh-and-blood-form, recasting the tractate by adding a sizable number of narratives.

I:I.1.
A. **Moses** was sanctified in a cloud and **received Torah at Sinai,**
B. as it is said, *And the glory of the Lord dwelled on Mount Sinai.*
C. *"[...and the cloud covered him for six days],* (Ex. 24:16), namely, Moses.
D. "so as to purify him.
E. "This was an event that took place after the Ten Commandments [were revealed]," the words of R. Yosé the Galilean.
F. And R. Aqiba says, *"And the cloud covered it for six days* refers to the mountain, not to Moses.
G. "[The six days] were counted from the beginning of the new month.
H. *"And on the seventh day he called to Moses out of the midst of the cloud* (Ex. 24:16) — this was to pay honor to Moses."

I:I.2. A. Said R. Nathan, "On what account was Moses held up all those six days, during which time the word did not come to rest on him? It was so that all of the food and drink that was in his belly should be consumed before the moment at which he was sanctified, so that he might become like one of the ministering angels."

B. Said R. Him R. Mattia b. Heresh, "My lord, they said only that it was so as to make him fearful, that he would accept the teachings of the Torah in awe, fear, dread, and trembling, as it is said, *Serve the Lord in fear, rejoice with trembling* (Ps. 2:11)."

Moses is portrayed as a ministering angel, and he is not a mere sage.

I:II.1. A. By means of Moses the Torah was given at Sinai,
B. as it is said, *And he wrote them down on two stone tablets and handed them over to me* (Deut. 5:19).
C. And it further says, *These are the ordinances, the laws, and the Torahs which the Lord set forth between himself and the children of Israel at Mount Sinai by means of Moses* (Lev. 26:46).
D. The Torah which the Holy One, blessed be he, gave to Israel he gave only by means of Moses, as it is said, *...between himself and the children of Israel.*
E. Moses had the merit of serving as the messenger between the children of Israel and the Omnipresent.

This is a different kind of Moses, he is now an agent and not a prophet or a sage. He is also classified as a priest.

I:II.2. A. It was Moses who prepared the lambs for the consecration of the priesthood and the oil for the anointing of the priest, and with it he anointed Aaron and his sons for all the seven days of the rite of consecration.
B. It was out of that oil that the high priests and kings were anointed.
C. It was Eleazar who burned the red cow for the preparation of purification-water [Num. 19], from the water of which unclean people were purified for generations to come.
D. Said R. Eliezer, "The measure of the importance of the former rite is great, for it applies for the generations to come [not only for the original occasion], for Aaron and his sons were sanctified with the anointing oil,
E. "as it is said, *And Aaron and his sons you will anoint and you will sanctify them to serve as priests for me* (Ex. 30:3)."

I:V.2. A. Another meaning of **be prudent in judgment.**
B. How so? This teaches that a person should be forbearing in his opinions and should not be too captious in sticking to his opinions, for whoever is captious in sticking to his opinions forgets his opinions.
C. For so we find in the case of Moses, our master, that when he was captious in sticking to his views, he forgot his learning.
D. Where do we find with respect to Moses, our master, that when he was captious in sticking to his views, he forgot his learning?

14. Moses in the Fathers According to Rabbi Nathan   73

E. As it is said, *And Eleazar the priest said to the men of the army, who had gone out to battle, "This is the law of the Torah which the Lord commanded Moses"* (Num. 31:22). "It was Moses whom he commanded, and not me whom he commanded, Moses, my father's brother, whom he commanded, and not me, whom he commanded."

F. And where do we find with respect to Moses, our master, that he was captious in sticking to his views?

G. Lo, it says in respect to the officers of the army, *And Moses was angry with the officers of the host, and Moses said to them, Have you saved all the women alive? [Remember, it was they who, in Balaam's departure, set about seducing the Israelites into disloyalty to the Lord that day at Peor, so that the plague struck the community of the Lord]* (Num. 31:14).

I:V.3. A. *[and Moses said to them, Have you saved all the women alive :]*

B. If so, why does Scripture say, *all the women*?

C. But this is the counsel which the wicked Balaam gave against Israel, as it is said, *And now, lo, I am going to my people. Come, and let me advise you concerning what this people will do to your people in the end of days* (Num. 24:14).

D. He said to him, "This people, whom you hate, is famished for food and parched for drink, and they have nothing to eat or drink except for manna alone. Go and set up stalls for them, and lay out food and drink for them, and station beautiful princesses in them, so that the people will commit whoredom to Baal Peor and fall by the hand of the Omnipresent."

E. Forthwith Balak went and did everything that the wicked Balaam had advised him.

F. Now see how the wicked Balaam made Israel lose twenty-four thousand men, as it is said, *And those who died in the plague were twenty-four thousand* (Num. 25:9).

G. And does that not yield an argument *a fortiori*:

H. Now if Moses, our master, the sage, the greatest of the great, the progenitor of all prophets, when he was too exacting in his opinion, forgot his learning, all the more so is that the rule for us!

I. This teaches that a person should be forbearing in his opinions and should not be captious in sticking to his opinions.

This is an exceptional exposition. [1] Moses is central — an active player.

[2] Glosses of the received Scriptures yield the principle that one should not be stubborn in holding to his opinions.

[3] Moses is the progenitor of all prophets.

[4] How else may we classify the figure of Moses if not as a sage in this document? He is like God,

I:VI.1.
A. **Make a fence for the Torah.**
B. And make a fence around your words,
C. just as [1] the Holy One, blessed be he, made a fence around his words, and [2] the first man made a fence around his words. [3] The Torah made a fence around its words. [4] Moses made a fence around his words. And so too [5] Job as well as [6] the prophets and [7] writings and [8] sages — all of them made a fence around their words.

I:VII.1.A. What is the fence that [1] the Holy One, blessed be he, made around his words?
B. Lo, [Scripture] says, *And all the nations will say, On what account did the Lord do thus to this land* (Deut. 29:24).
C. This teaches that it was entirely obvious before Him who by his word brought the world into being that the generations to come were destined to say this.
D. Therefore the Holy One, blessed be he, said to Moses, "Moses, write it that way, and leave it for the coming generations to say, *It was because they abandoned the covenant of the Lord* (Deut. 29:24), *And they went and worshipped other gods and bowed down to them, gods which they had not know and which had not been assigned to them* (Deut. 29:25)."
E. Lo, in this way you learn that the Holy One, blessed be he, paid out the reward of his creatures to the letter [lit.: through peace].

[1] Moses is an active player He is subject to an elaborate exposition.
[2] Moses is distinct from the prophets and sages.
[3] I see no pattern governing the portrait of Moses as prophet or sage.
[4] He is more than a sage or a holy man.

Moses is comparable in this composite to Adam and Eve and the snake.

II:II.1.A. What sort of fence did [4] Moses make around his words?
B. Lo, Scripture says, *And the Lord said to Moses, "Go to the people and sanctify them today and tomorrow"* (Ex. 19:10).
C. But that righteous man, Moses, did not wish to speak to Israel in the way in which the Holy One, blessed be he, had spoken to him. Rather, this is how he spoke with them: *Be ready against the third day; do not come near a woman* (Ex. 19:15).
D. [And as to the fence that Moses made around his words,] it was on his own that he added a third day.
E. For this is how Moses reasoned matters: "If a man goes near his wife and produces a drop of semen on the third day, they will be unclean, and the Israelites will turn out to receive from Mount Sinai the words of the Torah in a state of uncleanness. Therefore I shall add a third day so that a man may not go near his wife, and hence will not produce a drop of semen on the third day, so the

14. Moses in the Fathers According to Rabbi Nathan

people will be in a state of cultic cleanness, and the Israelites will turn out to receive from Mount Sinai the words of the Torah in a state of cleanness."

II:III.1 A. This is one of the matters which Moses carried out on his own volition, and his plan coincided with the plan of the Omnipresent.

B. He kept away from his wife, and his plan coincided with the plan of the Omnipresent.

C. He kept away from the tent of meeting, and his plan coincided with the plan of the Omnipresent.

D. He kept away from the tent of meeting, and his plan coincided with the plan of the Omnipresent.

II:III.2 A. He kept away from his wife, and his plan coincided with the plan of the Omnipresent.

B. How so? He reasoned in this way: "If concerning the Israelites, who are sanctified only for a brief moment, and who have been designated only so as to accept upon themselves the Ten Commandments from Mount Sinai, the Holy One, blessed be he, has instructed me, *Go to the people and sanctify them today and tomorrow* (Ex. 19:10), I, who am designated for that task every single day and every single hour, and do not know when [God] will speak with me, whether by day or by night, all the more so that I should separate from having sexual relations."

C. And his plan coincided with the plan of the Omnipresent.

D. [Rejecting this view,] R. Judah b. Batera says, "Moses separated from having sexual relations with his wife only when he was explicitly instructed to do so by the Almighty, for it is said, *With him do I speak mouth to mouth* (Num. 12:8).

E. "Mouth to mouth I made it explicit to him, 'Separate from having sexual relations with a woman,' and he did so."

F. And some say that Moses separated from having sexual relations with his wife only when he was explicitly instructed to do so by the Almighty, as it is said, *Go, say to them, Return you to your tents* (Deut. 5:27), and it is written, *But as for you, stay here by me* (Deut. 5:28).

G. He went back [following Goldin, p. 19] but he separated [from having sexual relations with his wife].

H. And his plan coincided with the plan of the Omnipresent.

II:III.3 A. He kept away from the tent of meeting, and his plan coincided with the plan of the Omnipresent.

B. How so? He reasoned in this way: "If my brother Aaron, who has been anointed with anointing oil and with a profusion of priestly vestments and who serves at the altar in those vestments in a state of sanctification, has been told by the Holy One, blessed be he, *Speak to your brother Aaron, that he not come at any unspecified time to the sanctuary* [but only at strictly regulated intervals] (Lev. 16:2), I, who have not been designated for that purpose, all the more so that I should take my leave of the tent of meeting."

C. He therefore kept away from the tent of meeting, and his plan coincided with the plan of the Omnipresent.

II:III.4 A. He broke the tablets, and his plan coincided with the plan of the Omnipresent.
B. How so? They tell: When Moses went up to the height to receive the tablets,
C. (which were inscribed and kept in readiness from the six days of creation, for it is said, *The tablets were the work of God, and the writing the writing of God, incised on the tablets* (Ex. 32:16) — do not read inscribed but rather freedom [from *harut* to *herut*] for whoever is occupied in the Torah, lo, in his own context he is a free man —)
D. at that moment the ministering angels were forming a conspiracy against Moses, saying, "Lord of the ages, *What is man, that you are mindful of him? and the son of man, that you think of him? Yet you have made him but little lower than the angels and have crowned him with glory and honor. You have made him to have dominion over the works of your hands, you have put all things under his feet, sheep and oxen, all of them, yes, and the beasts of the fields, the fowl of the air, and the fish of the sea* (Ps. 8:5-9),"
E. and so they kept up the talk against Moses, saying, "What sort of creature is this one, born of woman, who has come up to the height?"
F. So it is said, *You have ascended on high, you have led captivity captive, you have taken gifts* (Ps. 68:19).
G. He took the [tablets] and went down, greatly rejoicing. When, however, he saw that offense that the people committed through the making of the calf, he thought, "How shall I give them the tablets? [If I do so,] I shall impose on them the duty of carrying out most weighty religious duties, on which account I shall also impose on them the liability to the death penalty inflicted at the hand of Heaven, for so it is written in them, *You shall not have any god other than me* (Ex. 20:3)."
H. He went back, and the seventy elders saw him and ran after him. He took hold of one end of the tablets, and they took hold of one end of the tablets. The strength of Moses was greater than that of all the rest of them, as it is written, *And in all the mighty hand and in all the great terror which Moses wrought in the sight of all Israel* (Deut. 34:12).
I. He looked at the tablets and realized that the writing had floated up from them. He said, "How shall I gave the Israelites tablets on which there is nothing of substance? Rather, I shall take and break them." For it is said, *So I took hold of the two tablets and I threw them out of my two hands and broke them* (Deut. 9:17).
J. R. Yosé the Galilean says, "I shall make a parable for you. To what may the matter be likened? To the case of a mortal king, who said to his messenger, 'Go and betroth a pretty girl for me, one who is

pious, whose deeds are graceful.' The messenger went and betrothed such a woman. After he betrothed her, he went and found out that she committed an act of whoredom with another man. Forthwith he constructed an argument *a fortiori* on his own authority, saying, 'If now I give her a marriage-contract, it will turn out that I shall impose on her liability to the death penalty, and she will be removed from the possibility of marrying my lord for all time.'

K. "So Moses, that righteous man, constructed an argument *a fortiori* on his own authority, saying, How shall I give the Israelites these tablets? [If I do so,] I shall impose on them the duty of carrying out most weighty religious duties, on which account I shall also impose on them the liability to the death penalty inflicted at the hand of Heaven, for so it is written in them, *One who sacrifices to other gods, instead of the Lord alone, will be utterly wiped out* (Ex. 22:19). Rather, I shall take hold of these and shatter them, and [later on] the Israelites will revert to good conduct."

L. *And I broke them before your eyes* (Deut. 9:17):

M. "[I did so in your sight] lest the Israelites say, 'Where are those first tablets, which you brought down? The whole matter is nothing but a joke.'"

N. [Rejecting the entire line of argument from A onward,] R. Judah b. Betera says, "Moses broke the tablets only because he was explicitly instructed to do so from the mouth of the Almighty, as it is said, for it is said, *With him do I speak mouth to mouth* (Num. 12:8).

O. "Mouth to mouth I made it explicit to him, 'Break the tablets,' [and he did so]."

P. And some say that Moses broke the tablets only when he was explicitly instructed to do so by the Almighty, as it is said, *And I saw, and behold, you have sinned against the Lord your God* (Deut. 9:17). It says, *And I saw,* only because he saw that the writing had floated up from the tablets.

Q. And other say that Moses broke the tablets only when he was explicitly instructed to do so by the Almighty, as it is said, *And there they are as he commanded me* (Deut. 10:5). It says, *He commanded me* only because since he had been commanded to do so, he broke them.

R. R. Eleazar b. Azariah says, "Moses broke the tablets only when he was explicitly instructed to do so by the Almighty, as it is said, *which Moses did before the eyes of all Israel* (Deut. 34:12). Just as in that latter case Moses had been commanded and so did what he did, likewise here, it was because he had been commanded that he did what he did."

S. R. Aqiba says, "Moses broke the tablets only when he was explicitly instructed to do so by the Almighty, as it is said, *And I took hold of the two tablets* (Deut. 9:17). What someone takes hold of is what he can hold on to. This teaches that Moses as so told by the mouth of the Almighty and Moses hold on as it were to his creator."

T. R. Meir says, "Moses broke the tablets only when he was explicitly instructed to do so by the Almighty, as it is said, *which you broke* (Deut. 10:2). 'Good for you that you broke them!'"

The story about Moses and the tablets elaborates on Scripture's count. [1] Moses is an active player is different from sages or prophets, subject to an elaborate exposition.

[2] The exegetical proof-texts provide for the routine propositions of Moses, but Moses is distinct from the prophets and sages.

[3] The portrait of Moses as prophet or sage sets forth a systematic picture.

[4] Moses is more than a sage or a holy man.

IX:III.3

A. Miriam argued, "I too was subject to the word, and I did not cease having sexual relations with my husband."

B. Aaron argued, "I too was subject to the Word, and I did not cease having sexual relations with my wife. So too our forefathers were subject to the word, and they did not cease to have sexual relations with their wives.

C. "But he [Moses], because he is arrogant, has ceased to have sexual relations with his wife."

D. And they did not judge him in his presence but in his absence, and they did not judge him on the basis of certain knowledge but only on the basis of doubt.

E. For it was a matter of doubt whether or not [he had refrained from having sexual relations with his wife merely because] he was arrogant.

F. Now this yields an argument *a fortiori*: if Miriam, who spoke only against her brother, and who spoke only behind Moses' back, was punished, an ordinary person, who speaks ill of his fellow in his presence and humiliates him, all the more so will his punishment be considerable.

IX:III.4 A. At that time Aaron said to Moses, "Moses, my brother, is it your view that this leprosy afflicts only Miriam? It afflicts not her flesh alone but also our father, Amram.

B. "I shall give you a parable. To what may the matter be likened? It is like someone who put a coal into his hand. Even though he turns it this way and that, nonetheless his flesh is burned.

C. "For it is said, *Let her not, I ask, be as a corpse (Num.* 12:12)."

XII:I.3 A. Another comment on the same verse: Why did all the Israelites mourn for Aaron for thirty days [Goldin: while only the men wept for Moses]?

B. Because [following Goldin's insertions] Moses gave a strict judgment in accord with the truth, while Aaron never said to someone, "You have committed an offense," or to a woman, "You have committed an offense."

14. Moses in the Fathers According to Rabbi Nathan

  C. That is why *every member of the house of Israel wept for Aaron for thirty days*.

  D. But of Moses, who rebuked the people with harsh words, it is said, *And the sons of Israel mourned for Moses* (Deut. 34:8).

  E. And how many thousands of Israelites are called Aaron, for were it not for Aaron['s principles], this one would not have come into the world.

XII:I.4 A. And there are those who say that for this reason it is said *every member of the house of Israel wept for Aaron for thirty days:*

  B. Whoever can see our lord, Moses, standing and weeping and not join in the weeping?

XII:I.5 A. And there are those who say that for this reason it is said *every member of the house of Israel wept for Aaron for thirty days:*

  B. Whoever can see Eleazar and Phineas, sons of high priests, standing and weeping, and not join in the weeping?

XII:II.1 A. At that moment Moses asked for a death like the death of Aaron,

  B. for he saw the bier of Aaron lying in state in great honor, with bands of ministering angels lamenting for him.

  C. But did he ask for such a death in the presence of some other person? Was it not in the privacy of his own heart? But the Holy One, blessed be he, heard what he had whispered to himself.

  D. And how do we know that Moses asked for a death like the death of Aaron and [the Holy One, blessed be he,] heard what he had whispered to himself?

  E. As it is said, *Die in the mountain to which you go up, and be gathered to your people as Aaron your brother died in Mount Hor* (Deut. 32:50).

  F. Thus you have learned that Moses asked for a death like the death of Aaron.

XII:II.2 A. At that time [the Holy One, blessed be he] said to the angel of death, "Go, bring me the soul of Moses."

  B. The angel of death went and stood before him, saying to him, "Moses, give me your soul."

  C. Moses grew angry with him and said to him, Where I am sitting you have no right even to stand, yet you have said, 'Give me your soul'!" He threw him out with outrage.

  D. Then the Holy One, blessed be he, said to Moses, "Moses, you have had enough of this world, for lo, the world to come is readied for you, for a place is prepared for you from the first six days of creation."

  E. For it is said, *And the Lord said, Behold a place by me, and you shall stand upon the rock* (Ex. 33:21).

  F. The Holy One, blessed be he, took the soul of Moses and stored it away under the throne of glory.

  G. And when he took it, he took it only with a kiss, as it is said, *By the mouth of the Lord* (Deut. 34:5).

XII:II.3 A. It is not the soul of Moses alone that is stored away under the throne of glory, but the souls of the righteous are stored away under the throne of glory,

B. as it is said, *Yet the soul of my Lord shall be bound in the bundle of life with the Lord your God* (1 Sam. 25:29).

C. Is it possible to imagine that that is the case also with the souls of the wicked?

D. Scripture says, *And the souls of your enemies, those he shall sling out as from the hollow of a sling* (1 Sam. 25:29).

E. For even though one is tossed from place to place, it does not know on what to come to rest.

F. So too the souls of the wicked go roving and fluttering about the world and do not know where to come to rest.

XII:II.4 A. The Holy One, blessed be he, further said to the angel of death, ""Go, bring me the soul of Moses."

B. The angel of death went in search of him in his place but did not find him. He went to the Great Sea and said to it, "Has Moses come here?"

C. The sea replied, "From the day on which the Israelites passed through me, I have not seen him."

D. He went to the mountains and hills and said to them, "Has Moses come here?"

E. They replied, "From the day on which Israel received the Torah on Mount Sinai, we have not seen him.

F. He went to Sheol and Destruction and said to them, "Has Moses come here?"

G. They said to him, "His name we have heard, but him we have never seen."

H. He went to the ministering angels and said to them, "Has Moses come here?"

I. They said to him, "*God understands his way [and knows his place]*. God has hidden him away for the life of the world to come, and no one knows where."

J. So it is said, *But wisdom, where shall it be found? and where is the place of understanding? Man does not know its price, nor is it found in the land of the living. The deep says, It is not in me, and the sea says, It is not with me....Destruction and death say, We have heard a rumor thereof with our ears* (Job.28:13-15, 22).

XII:II.5 A. Joshua too was seated and grieving for Moses,

B. until the Holy One, blessed be he, said to him, "Joshua, why are you grieving for Moses? *Moses, my servant, is dead* (Joshua 1:2)."

The burial of Moses emphasizes his humility. He is central to the narrative, which stresses his exemplary conduct. He contrasts with his son in knowledge of the Torah.

14. Moses in the Fathers According to Rabbi Nathan

XVII:II.2

A. When Moses, our master, saw that his sons had no knowledge of the Torah, which would qualify them to succeed him in the leadership, he cloaked himself and stood in prayer.

B. He said before him, "Lord of the world, Tell me who will go in [and] who will come out at the head of all this people?"

C. For it is said, *And Moses spoke to the Lord, saying, Let the Lord, the God of the spirits of all flesh, set a man over the congregation, who may go out before them and who may come in before them* (Num. 27:15ff).

D. Said the Holy One, blessed be he, to Moses, *Moses, take Joshua* (Num. 27:15).

E. Said the Holy One, blessed be he, to Moses, "Go and act as his voice so that he may give an exposition in your presence at the head of all the great men of Israel [and that will signify that he is heir]."

F. At that moment Moses said to Joshua, "Joshua, As to this people that I am handing over to you, I am giving you not goats but kids, not sheep but lambs, for as yet they are not much experienced in the practice of religious duties, and they have not yet reached the growth of goats and sheep."

G. So it is said, *If you do not know, O you fairest among women, go your way forth by the footsteps of the flock and feed your kids beside the shepherds' tents* (Song 1:8).

IX:III.5

A. At that time Aaron began to appease Moses. He said to him, My brother, Moses, have we ever done ill to anyone in the world?"

B. He said to him, "No."

C. He said to him, "Now if we have never done ill to anyone in the world, how should we do evil to you, our brother! But what can I do? It was a mistake on our side! We neglected the covenant between you and us, as it is said, *And they did not remember the covenant of brothers* (Amos 1:9).

D. "On account of the covenant that has been drawn up between us, which we have neglected, shall we now lose our sister?"

E. At that moment Moses drew a little circle and stood in it and sought mercy for her, saying, "I am not going to move from here until you heal Miriam my sister," as it is said, *Let her not, I ask, be as a corpse* (Num. 12:12).

F. At that moment the Holy One, blessed be he, said to Moses, "If a king had grown angry against her, if her father had grown angry with her, she would have had to bear the shame for seven days. I, the King of kings of kings, all the more so is it not proper that she should bear her shame for fourteen days? But on your account, it will be forgiven to her."

G. So it is said, *And the Lord said to Moses, if her father should spit in her face* (Num. 12:14).

IX:III.6 A. *Now the man, Moses, was very meek, more than everyone on the face of the earth* (Num. 12:3):

B. Is it possible to suppose that he was meek in that he was a runt [lit.: not handsome and praiseworthy]?

C. Scripture says, *And he spread the tent of the tabernacle* (Ex. 40:19).

D. Just as the tabernacle was ten cubits high, so Moses was ten cubits tall.

E. Is it possible to suppose that he was [Goldin: more] meek than the ministering angels?

F. Scripture says, *...more than everyone on the face of the earth* (Num. 12:3).

G. They have said that he was more meek than men, not than ministering angels.

H. Is it possible to suppose that he was more meek than the ancients?

I. Scripture says, *...more than everyone on the face of the earth* (Num. 12:3), meaning, more than anyone in his generation, not more than the ancients.

J. There are three kinds of furunculars created in the world, moist, dry, and the polypus-kind, and Moses was more humble than any of them.

IX:IV.1 A. R. Simeon b. Eleazar says, "Also plagues come upon those who gossip, for so we find in the case of Gehazi, who gossiped against his master, that leprosy afflicted him until the day of his death."

B. For it is said, *The leprosy therefore of Naaman shall cleave to you...and he went out from his presence a leper as white as snow* (2 Kgs. 5:27).

C. He used to say, "Also plagues come upon those who are arrogant, for so we find in the case of Uzziah."

D. For it is said, *But when he was strong, his heart was lifted up so that he did corruptly, and he trespassed against the Lord his God, for he went into the temple of the Lord to burn incense upon the altar of incense. And Azariah the priest went in after him, and with him eighty priests of the Lord, valiant men, and they opposed King Uzziah and said to him, It is not your task, Uzziah, to burn incense to the Lord, but it is the priests' task, that of the sons of Aaron, who are consecrated, to burn the incense. Go out of the sanctuary, for you have committed sacrilege, neither is it for your honor from the Lord God. Uzziah was angry, and he had a censer in his hand to burn incense, and while he was angry with the priests, leprosy broke out on his forehead* (2 Chr. 26:16-19).

E. At that moment the sanctuary split in two, leaving a gap of twelve miles, and the priests quickly pushed him out: *Yes, he made haste to leave, because the Lord had smitten him. And he was a leper to the death of his death and dwelt in a house set apart as a leper, for he was cut off from the house of the Lord, and Jotham his son was in charge of the king's palace, judging the people of the land* (2 Chr. 26:20-21).

14. Moses in the Fathers According to Rabbi Nathan

The story about Moses's relationship with his family and about Moses's death is elaborately and originally expounded

[1] Moses is the key figure in this elaborate account.

[2] The account of Scripture is elaborated and refocused This is a remarkable execution.

[3-4] We identify a pronounced bias in the humility of Moses as to the death of Moses.

15

Moses in Yerushalmi Berakhot and Zeraim

A Talmud is formed of [1] the law code, the Mishnah, [2] the Gemara or Talmud, a commentary to the Mishnah, [3] The Gemara or Talmud to passages of the Tosefta, and [4] glosses of passages of the related Tannaite exegesis. There are two Talmuds, the Yerushalmi and the Bavli, the Talmud of the Land of Israel and the Talmud of Babylonia. The Talmud of the Land of Israel is comprised by five divisions and the one of Babylonia is made up of five divisions.

YERUSHALMI BERAKHOT

[I:8 A] [Regarding this [relationship between God and his people,] R. Yudan in the name of R. Isaac gave four discourses [in the form of parables]:

[B] [1] A person had a human patron. [One day] they came and told him [the patron], "A member of your household has been arrested."

[C] He said to them, "Let me take his place."

[D] They said to him, "Lo, he is already going out to trial."

[E] He said to them, "Let me take his place."

[F] They said to him, "Lo, he is going to be hanged."

[G] Now where is he and where is his patron [when ultimately he needs him]?

[H] But the Holy One, blessed be He, [will save his subjects, just as he] saved Moses from [execution by] the sword of Pharaoh.

[I] *This is in accord with what is written, 'He delivered me from the sword of Pharaoh'* [Ex. 18:4].

[J] Said R. Yannai, "It is written, 'Moses fled from Pharaoh' [Ex. 2:15]. Is it possible for a person to flee from the government? [No.] But when Pharaoh arrested Moses, he ordered that they decapitate him. But [when they tried to do so,] the sword bounced off Moses' neck and broke.

[K] "This accords with what is written, 'Your neck is like an ivory tower' [Song of Songs 7:4]. This refers to Moses' neck."

[L] Rabbi said, R. Abyatar [said], "Moreover, the sword bounced off neck, and it fell on Quaestionarius' [the executioner's] neck, and killed him. This accords with that which is written, 'He delivered me from the sword of Pharaoh' [Ex. 18:4]. He delivered me, and the executioner was killed."

[M] R. Berekhiah recited concerning [the story of this incident] the verse, "The ransom of the righteous is the wicked" [Prov. 21:18].

[N] R. Abun recited, "The righteous is delivered from trouble; and the wicked gets into it instead" [Prov. 11:8].

[O] *Taught Bar Qappara,* "An angel came down, and took Moses' appearance. And they arrested the angel, and Moses escaped."

[P] Said R. Joshua b. Levi, "When Moses fled from Pharaoh, all his people became either dumb, deaf, or blind. He said to the mute ones, 'Where is Moses?' And they could not speak. He asked the deaf ones, and they could not hear. He asked the blind ones, and they could not see.

[Q] "This accords with what the Holy One, blessed be He, said to Moses [when Moses was afraid to go before Pharaoh], 'Who has made a man's mouth? Who makes him dumb, or deaf, or seeing, or blind? Is it not I, the Lord?' [Ex. 4:11].

[R] "[God told Moses,] 'I saved you there [when you fled from Pharaoh]. Shall I not stand up for you now [when you go before Pharaoh to bring down the plagues on Egypt]?'

[S] "In this regard [the verse says], 'For what great nation is there that has a god so near to it as the Lord our God is to us, whenever we call upon him' [Deut. 4:7]."

[T] R. Yudan in the name of R. Isaac gave another discourse [in the form of a parable.] [2] A person had a human patron. [One day] they came and told the patron, "A member of your household has been arrested."

[U] He said, "Let me take his place."

[V] They said to him, "Lo, he is already going out to trial."

[W] He said to them, "Let me take his place."

[X] They said to him, "Lo, he is going to be thrown into the water [to be executed]."

[Y] Now where is he and where is his patron?

[Z] But the Holy One, blessed be He, [saves his subjects, just as he] saved Jonah from the belly of the fish. Lo it says, "And the Lord spoke to the fish, and it vomited out Jonah upon dry land" [Jonah 2:10].

[AA] R. Yudan in the name of R. Isaac gave another discourse [in the form of a parable.] [3] A person had a human patron. [One day] they came and told the patron, "A member of your household has been arrested."

[BB] He said to them, "Let me take his place."

[CC] They said to him, "He is going out to trial."
[DD] He said to them, "Let me take his place."
[EE] They said to him, "Lo, he is going to be thrown into the fire [to be executed]."
[FF] Now where is he and where is his patron?
[GG] But the Holy One, blessed be He, is not like that. He [saves his subjects, just as he] saved Haninah, Mishael and Azariah [Shadrach, Meshach, Abednego] from the fiery furnace.
[HH] In this regard [it says], "Nebuchadnezzar said, 'Blessed be the God of Shadrach, Meshach, and Abednego, [who has sent his angel and delivered his servants, who trusted in him]'" [Dan. 3:28].
[II] R. Yudan in the name of R. Isaac gave another discourse [in the form of a parable.] [4] A person had a human patron. [One day they came and told the patron, "A member of your household has been arrested."
[JJ] He said to them, "Let me take his place."
[KK] They said to him, "He is going out to trial."
[LL] He said to them, "Let me take his place."]
[MM] They said to him, "He is to be thrown to the beasts [to be executed]."
[NN] [Now where is he and where is his patron?]
[OO] But the Holy One, blessed by He, [saves his subjects, just as he] saved Daniel from the lions' den.
[PP] In this regard [it says], "My God sent his angels and shut the lions' mouths, and they have not hurt me" [Dan. 6:22].
[QQ] R. Yudan [gave another discourse in the form of a parable] in his own name: [5] A man has a human patron. When this man faces trouble, he does not suddenly burst in [on his patron to ask for help]. Rather he comes and stands at his patron's gate and calls to his patron's servant or some member of his household. And he [the servant] in turn informs the patron, "So and so is standing at the gate of your courtyard. Do you wish me to let him enter, or shall I let him stand outside?"
[RR] But the Holy One, blessed by He, is not like that. [God says,] "If a person faces trouble, he should not cry out to the angels Michael or Gabriel. But he should cry out to me and I will immediately answer him."
[SS] In this regard [it says], "All who call upon the name of the Lord shall be delivered" [Joel 2:32 RSV].
[TT] *Said R. Pinhas, "This incident occurred to Rab."*
[UU] *He was coming up from the hot spring of Tiberias. He met some Romans. They asked him, "Who are you?"*
[VV] *He said to them, "I am a member of [the governor] Severus' [entourage]." They let him pass.*
[WW] *That night they came to [the governor] and said to him, "How much longer will you put up with these Jews?"*
[XX] *He said to them, "What do you mean?"*

[YY] *They said to him, "We encountered a person. He said he was a Jew. We asked him who he was. And he said he was from Severus' [entourage]."*
[ZZ] *He [the governor] said to them, "What did you do for him?"*
[AAA] *They said to him, "Is it not enough that we let him alone?"*
[BBB] *He said to them, "You acted very well."*
[CCC] [The lesson of this story is:] One who relies on the protection of mere flesh and blood may be saved. How much more will one who relies on the protection of the Holy One, blessed be He, [be saved from harm].

[1] Is Moses an active player or a routine and scarcely animate one? Moses is at the forefront of the narrative, which is well organized and focused,

[2] What components of the collection make routine glosses of the received Scriptures and which ones provide more than minor glosses of the tradition? These are not random items but well organized and carefully focused

[3] Can we identify a pronounced bias or a polemical program in the unfolding entries that transform Moses the prophet and king of Israel into Rabbi Moses? The program emphasizes the humility of Moses, which predominates throughout.

[4] The account centers on the virtue of Moses. But we could easily substitute any other human being for Moses and emerge with the same repertoire of virtues.

16

Moses in Yerushalmi Moed

YERUSHALMI TAANIT

[I:1 A] It is written, "The glory of the Lord settled on Mount Sinai, *and the cloud covered it six days; and* on the seventh *day* he called to Moses out of the midst of the cloud" (Ex. 2:16). [And it also says] "and Moses went up…(Ex. 2:15)."

[B] This was the seventh day after the declaration of the Ten Commandments, and the beginning of the forty [days that Moses spent on the mountain]. [On the sixth of Sivan the Torah was given, and on the next day began the forty days that Moses spent on the mountain.]

[C] Said Moses to the people, *"I am going to spend forty days on the mountain."*

[D] When the fortieth day came, and he did not come down, then: "When the people saw that Moses delayed to come down from the mountain, [the people gathered themselves together to Aaron and said to him, 'Up, make us gods who shall go before us…']" (Ex. 32:1).

[E] When the sixth hour had passed, and he did not come down, thereupon: "The people gathered themselves together to Aaron and said to him. 'Up, make us gods who will go before us'" (Ex. 32:1)

[F] "And the Lord said [68c] to .Moses, 'Go down, for your people, [whom you brought up out of the land of Egypt], have corrupted themselves'" (Ex. 32:7).

[G] "When Joshua heard the noise of the people in their wickedness, he said to Moses, 'There is a noise of war in the camp'" (Ex. 32:17).

[H] Said Moses, "Here is a man who is destined to govern 600,000 people, yet he does not know the difference between one sort of noise and another!"

[I] "He said, 'It is not the sound of shouting for victory or the sound of the cry of defeat, but the sound of singing that I hear'" (Ex. 32:18).

[J] Said R. Yosé, "'It is the sound of praise of idols that I hear.'"

[K] Said R. Yudan in the name of R. Yosé, "There is not a generation in which a particular of the sin of the worship of the calf is not [to be atoned for through suffering]."

[L] "And as soon as he came near the camp and saw the calf and the dancing" (Ex. 32:19).

[M] R. Hilqiah in the name of R. Aha: "It is on the basis of this story [in which Moses does not break the tablets until he actually sees what is going on, despite the good guess on the basis of the sounds he hears], that we learn that one should not reach a judgment on the basis of guesswork."

[N] Moses made the following interpretation on the basis of an argument a fortiori: "Now if in the case of the Passover lamb, which is a single religious duty, it is stated, '[And when a stranger shall sojourn with you and would keep the passover to the Lord, let all his males be circumcised, then he may come near and keep it; he shall be as a native of the land.] But no uncircumcised person shall eat of it' (Ex. 12:8).

[O] "as to the Torah, in which all the religious duties are contained — is it not an argument a *fortiori* [that these people are unworthy to receive it]?"

[P] "[And as soon as he came near the camp and saw the calf and the dancing], Moses' anger burned hot, and he threw the tables out of his hands and broke them at the foot of the mountain" (Ex. 32:19).

[Q] *R. Ishmael taught,* "The Holy One, blessed be he, told him to break them, for it is said, 'And I will write on the tables the words that were on the first tables which you broke, and you shall put them in the ark'" (Deut. 10:2).

[R] He said to him, "You did the right thing in breaking them."

[S] R. Samuel bar Nahman in the name of R. Jonathan: "The tablets were six handbreadths long and three broad. Moses was holding on to two handbreadths, and the Holy One, blessed be he, was holding on to two of them, and there was a space of two hand(breadths in the middle.

[T] "When the Israelites did their deed. the Holy One, blessed be he, wanted to grab them out of the hand of Moses. But the hand of Moses was stronger and he seized them from him.

[U] "That is in line with what Scripture says in praising Moses at the end, saying, 'And for all the mighty power [the Hebrew word for power also means hand] [and all the great and terrible deeds which Moses wrought in the sight of all Israel]' (Deut. 34:12).

[V] *"[It is as if God then says,] 'Let there be peace unto the hand that was stronger than mine.'"*

16. Moses in Yerushalmi Moed

[W] R. Yohanan in the name of R. Yosé bar Abbayye said to him, "The tablets wanted to fly, but Moses was holding on to them, as it is written, 'So I took hold of the two tables, [and cast them out of my two hands, and broke them before your eyes]'" (Deut . 9:17) .

[X] *It was taught in the name of R. Nehemiah,* "The writing itself flew off [the tablets]."

[Y] R. Ezra in the name of R. Judah b. R. Simon: "The tablets were a burden weighing forty *seahs,* and the writing was holding them up. When the writing flew off, the tablets became heavy on the hands of Moses, and the tablets fell and were broken."

[1] Is Moses an active player or a routine and scarcely animate one? Moses stands at the heart of the exposition and his role is active.

[2] What components of the collection make routine glosses of the received Scriptures and which ones provide more than minor glosses of the tradition? The failure to keep to the time limit of forty days marks the major glosses of the narrative.

[3] Moses could not hold up the tablets.

[4] How is Moses comparable to sages in this document? How else may we classify the figure of Moses if not as a sage in this document? Moses is the central figure in the narrative.

YERUSHALMI TAANIT 2:5

[A] **For the second he says, "He who answered our fathers at the Red Sea will answer you and hear the sound of your cry this day. Blessed are you, O Lord, who remembers forgotten things."**

[I:1 A] At the sea our fathers were divided into four parties.

[B] One of them said, "Let us throw ourselves into the sea."

[C] One of them said, "Let us go back to Egypt."

[D] One of them said, "Let us fight against them."

[E] And one of them said, "Let us cry out against them."

[F] To this one which said, "Let us fall into the sea," Moses said, "Fear not, stand firm, and see the salvation of the Lord, [which he will work for you today; for the Egyptians whom you see today, you shall never see again]" (Ex. 14:13).

[G] To the one which said, "Let us go back to Egypt," Moses said, "[Fear not, stand firm, and see the salvation of the Lord, which he will work for you today]; for the Egyptians whom you see today, [you shall never see again]" (Ex. 14:13).

[H] To the one which said, "Let us fight against them," Moses said, "The Lord will fight for you [and you have only to be still]" (Ex. 14:14).

[I] To the one which said, "Let us cry out against them," Moses said, "And you have only to be still" (Ex. 14:14).

[1] Is Moses an active player or a routine and scarcely animate one? Moses argues with the Israelites, answering the polemics as they unfold.

[2] What components of the collection make routine glosses of the received Scriptures and which ones provide more than minor glosses of the tradition? The entire exposition traces Moses's active engagement in polemics against the enemies of God.

[3] Moses is not a sage or a wonder worker but takes up a unique role n the polemic with the people.

[4] How is Moses comparable to sages in this document? Moses is neither sage nor wonder worker but principal voice of God[s will. How else may we classify the figure of Moses if not as a sage in this document?

YERUSHALMI TAANIT 2:6

[I:1A] It is written, "The glory of the Lord settled on Mount Sinai, *and the cloud covered it six days; and* on the seventh *day* he called to Moses out of the midst of the cloud" (Ex. 2:16). [And it also says] "and Moses went up...(Ex. 2:15)."

[B] This was the seventh day after the declaration of the Ten Commandments, and the beginning of the forty [days that Moses spent on the mountain]. [On the sixth of Sivan the Torah was given, and on the next day began the forty days that Moses spent on the mountain.]

[C] Said Moses to the people, *"I am going to spend forty days on the mountain."*

[D] When the fortieth day came, and he did not come down, then: "When the people saw that Moses delayed to come down from the mountain, [the people gathered themselves together to Aaron and said to him, 'Up, make us gods who shall go before us...']" (Ex. 32:1).

[E] When the sixth hour had passed, and he did not come down, thereupon: "The people gathered themselves together to Aaron and said to him. 'Up, make us gods who will go before us'" (Ex. 32:1)

[F] "And the Lord said [68c] to .Moses, 'Go down, for your people, [whom you brought up out of the land of Egypt], have corrupted themselves'" (Ex. 32:7).

[G] "When Joshua heard the noise of the people in their wickedness, he said to Moses, 'There is a noise of war in the camp'" (Ex. 32:17).

[H] Said Moses, "Here is a man who is destined to govern 600,000 people, yet he does not know the difference between one sort of noise and another!"

[I] "He said, 'It is not the sound of shouting for victory or the sound of the cry of defeat, but the sound of singing that I hear'" (Ex. 32:18).

[J] Said R. Yosé, "'It is the sound of praise of idols that I hear.'"

[K] Said R. Yudan in the name of R. Yosé, "There is not a generation in which a particular of the sin of the worship of the calf is not [to be atoned for through suffering]."

16. Moses in Yerushalmi Moed   93

[L] "And as soon as he came near the camp and saw the calf and the dancing" (Ex. 32:19).

[M] R. Hilqiah in the name of R. Aha: "It is on the basis of this story [in which Moses does not break the tablets until he actually sees what is going on, despite the good guess on the basis of the sounds he hears], that we learn that one should not reach a judgment on the basis of guesswork."

[N] Moses made the following interpretation on the basis of an argument a fortiori: "Now if in the case of the Passover lamb, which is a single religious duty, it is stated, '[And when a stranger shall sojourn with you and would keep the passover to the Lord, let all his males be circumcised, then he may come near and keep it; he shall be as a native of the land.] But no uncircumcised person shall eat of it' (Ex. 12:8).

[O] "as to the Torah, in which all the religious duties are contained — is it not an argument a *fortiori* [that these people are unworthy to receive it]?"

[P] "[And as soon as he came near the camp and saw the calf and the dancing], Moses' anger burned hot, and he threw the tables out of his hands and broke them at the foot of the mountain" (Ex. 32:19).

[Q] *R. Ishmael taught,* "The Holy One, blessed be he, told him to break them, for it is said, 'And I will write on the tables the words that were on the first tables which you broke, and you shall put them in the ark'" (Deut. 10:2).

[R] He said to him, "You did the right thing in breaking them."

[S] R. Samuel bar Nahman in the name of R. Jonathan: "The tablets were six handbreadths long and three broad. Moses was holding on to two handbreadths, and the Holy One, blessed be he, was holding on to two of them, and there was a space of two hand(breadths in the middle.

[T] "When the Israelites did their deed. the Holy One, blessed be he, wanted to grab them out of the hand of Moses. But the hand of Moses was stronger and he seized them from him.

[U] "That is in line with what Scripture says in praising Moses at the end, saying, 'And for all the mighty power [the Hebrew word for power also means hand] [and all the great and terrible deeds which Moses wrought in the sight of all Israel]' (Deut. 34:12).

[V] *"[It is as if God then says,] 'Let there be peace unto the hand that was stronger than mine.'"*

[W] R. Yohanan in the name of R. Yosé bar Abbayye said to him, "The tablets wanted to fly, but Moses was holding on to them, as it is written, 'So I took hold of the two tables, [and cast them out of my two .Moses, and the tablets fell and were broken."

[1] Is Moses an active player or a routine and scarcely animate one? Moses is the principal actor in the narrative.

[2] What components of the collection make routine glosses of the received Scriptures and which ones provide more than minor glosses of the tradition? Moses drives the narrative forward.

[3] Can we identify a pronounced bias or a polemical program in the unfolding entries that transform Moses the prophet and king of Israel into Rabbi Moses? Or are the entries that clarify Scripture through the contrast with tradition scattered without pattern in the Rabbinic canon? There is nothing random in the narrative, the events reveal a pattern.

[4] How is Moses comparable to sages in this document? How else may we classify the figure of Moses if not as a sage in this document? Moses is a unique figure.

[I:3 A] R. Samuel bar Nahman in the name of R. Jonathan: "Eighty five elders, and among them some thirty-odd prophets, were troubled about this matter. They said, 'It is written, "These are the commandments which the Lord commanded Moses for the people of Israel on Mount Sinai' (Lev. 27:34). These then are the commandments which we have received from the mouth of Moses.

[B] "And thus did Moses say to us, 'No other prophet is going to make anything new for you. Now here are Mordecai and Esther, who want to make something new for us.'

[C] "They did not move from that place, debating the matter, until the Holy One, blessed be he, enlightened their eyes, so they found support for the proposition written in the Torah, Prophets, and Writings."

[D] *It is in line with that which is written,* "And the Lord said to Moses, 'Write this as a memorial in a book [and recite it in the ears of Joshua, that I will utterly blot out the remembrance of Amalek from under heaven'"] (Ex. 17:14).

[E] "This" refers to the Torah, as it is written, "And this is the Torah that Moses placed before the Israelites (Deut. 4:44).

[F] "Memorial" refers to the prophets: ["Then those who feared the Lord spoke with one another; the Lord heeded and heard them,] and a book of remembrance was written before him of those who feared the Lord and thought on his name" (Mal. 3:16).

[G] "In a book" refers to the writings: "The command of Queen Esther fixed these practices of Purim, and it was recorded in a book" (Est. 9:32).

[H] Rab, R. Haninah, R. Jonathan, Bar Qappara, R. Joshua b. Levi said, "This scroll was stated to Moses at Sinai, for there are no considerations of chronology [or anachronism] in the Torah."

[1] Is Moses an active player or a routine and scarcely animate one? Moses is subjected to a disciplined exegesis.

16. Moses in Yerushalmi Moed

[2] What components of the collection make routine glosses of the received Scriptures and which ones provide more than minor glosses of the tradition? The composition is comprised by Scripture and its narrative of Moses.

[3] The exposition relies on Scripture for the bulk of the treatment.

[4] How is Moses comparable to sages in this document? He is similar to any other sage.

Moses is comparable to any sage. The composites of Yerushalmi Moed portrays Moses as a standard rabbinic figure.

17

Moses in Yerushalmi Nashim

Nothing weighty presents itself.

18

Moses in Yerushalmi Neziqin

YERUSHALMI SANHEDRIN

[II:1A] An Epicurean [M. San. 10:1D(3)]: ." .]

[II:2A] Rab said, "Korach was very rich. [The location of] Pharaoh's treasures was revealed to him, between Migdal and the sea." [This item breaks off here.]

[B] Rab said, "Korach was an Epicurean. What did he do? He went and made a prayer shawl which was entirely purple [although the law is that only the fringe was to be purple]."

[C] He went to Moses, saying to him, "Moses, our rabbi: A prayer shawl which is entirely purple, what is the law as to its being liable to show fringes?"

[D] He said to him, "It is liable, for it is written, 'You shall make yourself tassels [on the four corners of your cloak with which you cover yourself]'" (Deut. 22:12).

[E] [Korach continued,] "A house which is entirely filled with holy books, what is the law as to its being liable for a *mezuzah* [containing sacred scripture, on the doorpost]?"

[F] He said to him, "It is liable for a *mezuzah,* for it is written, 'And you shall write them on the doorposts of your house [and upon your gates]'" (Deut. 6:9).

[G] He said to him, "A bright spot the size of a bean — what is the law [as to whether it is a sign of uncleanness in line with Lev. 13:2ff.]?"

[H] He said to him, "It is a sign of uncleanness."

[I] "And if it spread over the whole of the man's body?"

[J] He said to him, "It is a sign of cleanness."

[K] [28a] At that moment Korach said, "The Torah does not come from Heaven, Moses is no prophet, and Aaron is not a high priest."

[L] Then did Moses say, "Lord of all worlds, if from creation the earth was formed with a mouth, well and good, and if not, then make it now!

[M] "'But if the Lord creates [something new, and the ground opens its mouth, and swallows them up, with all that belongs to them, and they go down alive to Sheol, then you shall know that these men have despised the Lord]' (Num. 16:30)."

[II:3A] Said R. Simeon b. Laqish, "Three denied their prophetic gift on account of the baseness [with which they were treated].

[B] "And these are they: Moses, Elijah, and Micha."

[C] Moses said, "If these men die the common death of all men, [or if they are visited by the fate of all men, then the Lord has not sent me]" (Num. 16:29).

[D] Elijah said, "Answer me, O Lord, answer me, [that this people may know that thou, O Lord, art God, and that thou hast turned their hearts back]" (1 Kings 18:37).

[E] Micah said, "[And Micaiah said,] 'If you return in peace, the Lord has not spoken by me.' [And he said, 'Hear, all you peoples!']" (1 Kings 22:28).

[F] "So they and all that belonged to them went down alive into Sheol; [and the earth closed over them, and they perished from the midst of the assembly]" (Num. 16:33).

[1] Is Moses an active player or a routine and scarcely animate one? Moses is party to polemics,

[2] What components of the collection make routine glosses of the received Scriptures and which ones provide more than minor glosses of the tradition? The glosses are entirely standard,

[3] Can we identify a pronounced bias or a polemical program in the unfolding entries that transform Moses the prophet and king of Israel into Rabbi Moses? Moses proves superior to the prophets.

[4] How is Moses comparable to sages in this document? Moses is comparable to the sages but is superior to them.

HORAYOT

YERUSHALMI HORAYOT 3:1

[I:3 A] R. Joshua b. Levi said, "[If there] are a head [not a sage] and an elder [a sage], the elder takes precedence. For there is no head if there is no elder."

[B] *What is the scriptural evidence for this position?*

[C] "You stand this day all of you before the Lord your God: the heads of your tribes, your elders, and your officers, all the men of Israel (Deut. 29:10)."

18. Moses in Yerushalmi Neziqin

[D] And it is written, "Then Joshua gathered all the tribes of Israel to Shechem, and summoned the elders, the heads, the judges, and the officers of Israel (Joshua 24:1)."

[E] Thus Moses gave precedence to the heads over the elders, while Joshua gave precedence to the elders over the heads.

[F] Moses, because all of them were his disciples, gave precedence to the heads over the elders. Joshua, because all of them were not his disciples, gave precedence to the elders [who were sages] over the heads [who were not sages].

[G] Moses, because he did not then have need of their help in [48c] conquering the land, gave precedence to the heads over the elders. Joshua, because he then needed them for conquering the land, gave precedence to the elders over the heads.

[H] Moses, because he was not fatigued by the study of the Torah [having divine help], gave precedence to the heads over the elders. Joshua, because he was fatigued by study of the Torah, gave precedence to the elders over the heads.

[I] R. Joshua of Sikhnin in the name of R. Levi: "Moses, because he foresaw through the Holy Spirit that the Israelites were destined to be imprisoned by the [gentile] kingdoms, and their heads would be standing over them [to deal with the gentiles], gave precedence to the heads over the elders."

[1] Is Moses an active player or a routine and scarcely animate one? Moses is an active player in the succession.

[2] What components of the collection make routine glosses of the received Scriptures and which ones provide more than minor glosses of the tradition? Reasons are given to sustain Moses's position over that of the sages,

[3] The entries that clarify Scripture through the contrast with tradition are scattered without pattern in the Rabbinic canon.

[4] How is Moses comparable to sages in this document? Moses gives reasons for his positions.

Moses is an example of logic and is a model for sages. He explains the logical foundation for his positions and shows other sages the way forward.

19

Moses in Bavli Berakhot

BAVLI BERAKHOT CHAPTER FIVE

I.31 A. "And I will make of you a great nation" (Ex. 32:10):
B. Said R. Eleazar, "Said Moses before the Holy One, blessed be he, 'Lord of the age, Now if a stool with three legs cannot stand against you when you are angry, a stool with only one leg [that is, Moses] surely should not be able to stand!
C. "'Not only so, but I have to be ashamed before my forefathers, for now they will say, "See how the provider whom he set up over them seeks greatness for himself and does not seek mercy for them!"'"

I.32 A. "And Moses besought the Lord his God" (Ex. 32:11):
B. Said R. Eleazar, "This verse teaches that Moses stood in prayer before the Holy One, blessed be he, until he had exhausted him."
C. And Rab said, "It was until he had released him from his vow.
D. "Here it is written, 'He besought, and [in connection with vows], he shall not break his word ' [using the same verb] (Num. 30:3).
E. "And a master has said, 'He cannot break the vow, but others may break the vow for him.' [Moses thus released God 's vow.]"
F. And Samuel said, "This verse teaches that he gave himself up to death in their behalf.
G. "For it is said, 'And if not, blot me, I pray you, out of the book which you have written ' (Ex. 32:32)."
H. Raba said in the name of R. Isaac, "This verse teaches that he made the attribute of mercy rest on them."
I. And rabbis say, "This verse teaches that Moses said before the Holy One, blessed be he, 'Lord of the age, it would be perfectly common of you to do such a thing.'"
J. "And Moses besought the Lord" (Ex. 32:11):

K. *It has been taught on Tannaite authority:*
L. R. Eliezer the elder says, "This verse teaches that Moses stood in prayer before the Holy One, blessed be he, until he was seized by a fever."
M. *What is this fever?*
N. Said R. Eleazar, "It is a burning in the bones."

I.34 A. "And said to them, I will multiply your seed as the stars of heaven and all this land of which I have spoken" (Ex. 32:13):
B. This expression, "Of which I have spoken" should be "of which you have spoken"!
C. Said R. Eleazar, "Up to this point we have the words of the disciple [Moses]. From this point forward we have the words of the master [God]."
D. And R. Samuel bar Nahman said, "Both clauses are the words of the disciple. But this is what Moses said before the Holy One, blessed be he, 'Lord of the world, As to the words that you have spoken to me, telling me to go and say them to the Israelites in my name, indeed I did go and speak to them in your name. Now what shall I say to them.'"

I.35 A. "Because the Lord was not able" (Num. 14:16):
B. *[Since the word for "able" is given in the feminine form, it is asked,] Should not the word be given in the masculine form?*
C. Said R. Eleazar, "Said Moses before the Holy One, blessed be he, 'Lord of the age, now the nations of the world will say that his strength has become weak like a woman's, so he cannot save [them].'
D. "Said the Holy One, blessed be he, to Moses, 'But did they not already see the miracles and mighty deeds which I did for them at the sea?'
E. "He said to him, 'Lord of the age, But they still can say, "Against a single king he can stand, but against thirty-one kings he cannot stand."'"

F. Said R. Yohanan, "How do we know that the Holy One, blessed be he, retracted and conceded that Moses was right?
G. "As it is said, 'And the Lord said, I have pardoned according to your word' (Ex. 32:20)."
H. *On Tannaite authority in the house of R. Ishmael:* "'In accord with your word' (Ex. 32:20):
I. "The nations of the world are going to say this:' Happy is the disciple with whom his master concurs.'"

I.36 A. "But in very deed, as I live" (Ex. 32:21):
B. Said Raba said R. Isaac, "This teaches that the Holy One, blessed be he, said to Moses, 'Moses, you have given me life through your words.'"

19. Moses in Bavli Berakhot

I.37 A. R. Simlai expounded, "A person should always lay out words of praise for the Holy One, blessed be he, first of all, and then he should say the Prayer.
  B. "How do we know it?
  C. "It is from Moses, for it is written, 'And I besought the Lord at that time ' (Deut. 3:23).
  D. "And then it says, 'O Lord God, you have begun to show your servant your greatness and your strong hand, for what god is there in heaven and earth who can do according to your deeds and according to your mighty acts,' and then it is written, 'Let me go over, I pray you, and see the good land' (Deut. 3:23ff.).

[1] Is Moses an active player or a routine and scarcely animate one? Moses gave God life through his words, and in more general terms is an active participant.

[2] What components of the collection make routine glosses of the received Scriptures and which ones provide more than minor glosses of the tradition? This composite is formed by a long sequence of glosses,

[3] Can we identify a pronounced bias or a polemical program in the unfolding entries that transform Moses the prophet and king of Israel into Rabbi Moses? Or are the entries that clarify Scripture through the contrast with tradition scattered without pattern in the Rabbinic canon? The volume of exegeses is formidable but the upshot is familiar.

[4] How is Moses comparable to sages in this document? How else may we classify the figure of Moses if not as a sage in this document? There is no such option.

20

Moses in Bavli Moed

BAVLI ERUBIN

9:4 **I.41** A. And said R. Joshua b. Levi, "When Moses came up on high, the ministering angels said before the Holy One, blessed be He, 'Lord of the world, what is one born of woman doing among us?' He said to them, 'He has come to receive the Torah.'

B. "They said before him, 'This secret treasure, hidden by you for nine hundred and seventy-four generations before the world was created, are you now planning to give to a mortal? "What is man, that you are mindful of him, and the son of man, that you think of him, O Lord our God, how excellent is your name in all the earth! who has set your glory upon the heavens" (Ps. 8:5, 2)!'

C. "Said the Holy One, blessed be He, to Moses, 'Answer them.'

D. "He said before him, 'Lord of the world, I'm afraid lest they burn me with the breath of their mouths.'

E. "He said to him, 'Hold on to my throne of glory and answer them.' So Scripture says, 'He makes him to hold on to the face of his throne and spreads his cloud over him' (Job 26:9)." And in this connection R. Tanhum said, "This teaches that the All-Mighty spread over him some of the splendor of his Presence and his cloud."

F. "He said to him, 'Lord of the world, the Torah that you are giving me — what is written in it?'

G. "'I am the Lord your God who brought you out of the land of Egypt' (Ex. 20:2).

H. "He said to the angels, 'To Egypt have you gone down. To Pharaoh have you been enslaved? Why should the Torah go to you?'

I. "He again said to him, 'Lord of the world, the Torah that you are giving me — what is written in it?'

J. "'You will have no other gods' (Ex. 20:3).
K. "'So do you live among the nations who worship [89A] idols?'
L. "He again said to him, 'Lord of the world, the Torah that you are giving me — what is written in it?'
M. "'Remember the Sabbath day to keep it holy' (Ex. 20:8).
N. "'So do you do work that you need rest?'
O. "He again said to him, 'Lord of the world, the Torah that you are giving me — what is written in it?'
P. "'You shall not take the name of the Lord your god in vain' (Ex. 20:7).
Q. "'So is there any give or take among you?'
R. "He again said to him, 'Lord of the world, the Torah that you are giving me — what is written in it?'
S. "'Honor your father and your mother' (Ex. 20:12).
T. "'So do you have fathers and mothers?'
U. "He again said to him, 'Lord of the world, the Torah that you are giving me — what is written in it?'
V. "'You shall not murder, you shall not commit adultery, you shall not steal' (Ex. 20:13-15).
W. "'So is there envy among you, is there lust among you?'
X. "Forthwith they gave praise to the Holy One, blessed be He: 'O Lord our God, how excellent is your name' (Ps. 8:10), but they didn't add, 'who has set your glory upon the heavens.'
Y. "On the spot everyone of them became a friend of his and gave him something: 'You have ascended on high, you have taken the spoils, you have received gifts on account of man' (Ps. 68:19). In reparation for their calling you a man, you received gifts.
Z. "So, too, the angel of death handed over something to him: 'and he put on the incense and made atonement for the people' (Num. 16:47), 'and he stood between the dead and the living' (Num. 16:48). *If the other hadn't told him where, would he have known what to do?"*

I.42 A. And said R. Joshua b. Levi, "When Moses came down from before the Holy One, blessed be He, Satan came and said before him, 'Lord of the world, where is the Torah?'
B. "He said to him, 'I gave it to the earth.'
C. "He went to the earth and said to her, 'Where is the Torah?'
D. "'God understands her way' (Job 28:23).
E. "He went to the sea, and it replied, 'It is not with me.'
F. "He went to the deep, and it replied, 'It is not in me,' for it is said, 'The deep says, it is not in me, and the sea says, it is not with me, destruction and death say, we have heard a rumor thereof with our ears' (Job 28:14, 22).
G. "So he went back and said before the Holy One, blessed be He, 'Lord of the world, I have searched throughout the earth but not found it.'
H. "He said to him, 'Go to the Son of Amram.'

20. Moses in Bavli Moed

I. "He went to Moses. He said to him, 'The Torah that the Holy One, blessed be He, gave you — where is it?'

J. "He said to him, 'So what am I, that the Holy One, blessed be He, gave me the Torah?'

K. "Said the Holy One, blessed be He, to Moses, 'Moses, you're a liar!'

L. "He said before him, 'Lord of the world, you have a precious thing stored up for yourself, with which you play every day. Am I going to hold on to the benefit of that for myself?'

M. "Said the Holy One, blessed be He, to Moses, 'Since you have humbled yourself, it will be called by your name: "Remember you the Torah of Moses, my servant"' (Mal. 3:22)."

I.43 A. And said R. Joshua b. Levi, "At the time that Moses went up on high, he found the Holy One in session, affixing crowns to the letters [of the words of the Torah]. He said to him, 'Moses, don't people greet each other "peace" where you come from?'

B. "He said to him, 'Is there a servant who greets his master before the other greets him?'

C. "He said to him, 'You should have helped me right away.'

D. "He said to him, '"And now I pray you let the power of the Lord be great, according as you have spoken" (Num. 14:17).'"

I.44 A. And said R. Joshua b. Levi, "What is the meaning of the statement, 'And when the people saw that Moses delayed coming down from the mountain' (Ex. 32:1)? Read the word for delay as though its consonants yielded the word 'the sixth hour has come.'

B. "For when Moses went up on high, he said to the Israelites, 'At the end of forty days, at the beginning of the sixth hour, I shall come.' But at the end of forty days Satan came along and confounded the world.

C. "He said to them, 'As to Moses, your lord, where is he?'

D. "They said to him, 'He went up on high.'

E. "He said to them, 'It is now the sixth hour.' But they paid no attention to him.

F. "'He's dead.' But they paid no attention to him.

G. "He showed them a vision of his bier, and that is in line with what they said to Aaron, 'for this man, Moses...' (Ex. 32:1)."

I.45 A. *Said one of the rabbis to R. Kahana, "Have you heard the meaning of the words 'Mount Sinai'?"*

B. He said to him, "The mountain on which miracles [nissim] were done for Israel."

C. *"But then the name should be, Mount Nisai."*

D. "Rather, the mountain on which a good omen was done for Israel."

E. *"But then the name should be, Mount Sinai."*

F. *He said to him, "So why don't you hang out at the household of R. Pappa and R. Huna b. R. Joshua, for they're the ones who really look into lore."*

G. *For both of them say, "What is the meaning of the name, Mount Sinai? It is the mountain from which hatred descended for the gentiles."*

I.46 A. *That is in line with what* R. Yosé b. R. Hanina said, "It has five names: the wilderness of Sin, for there the Israelites were given commandments; the wilderness of Kadesh, where the Israelites were sanctified; the wilderness of Kedemot, for there the Israelites were given priority; the wilderness of Paran, **[89B]** for there Israel was fruitful and multiplied; and the wilderness of Sinai, for there hatred descended for the gentiles. But what really is its name? Horeb is its name."

B. *He differs from R. Abbahu, for* said R. Abbahu, "It is really called Mount Sinai, but why is it called Mount Horeb? Because there desolation descended on the gentiles."

II.1 A. **"How do we know that they tie a red thread on the head of the scapegoat [which is sent forth]? Since it says, 'Though your sins be as scarlet, they shall be white as snow' (Isa. 1:18)":**

B. *Rather than* "like scarlet threads," *what is needed is* "like a scarlet thread"!

C. Said R. Isaac, "Said the Holy One, blessed be He, to Israel, 'If your sins are like these years, which have continued in proper order all the way back from the six days of creation to the present, they still will be as white as snow.'"

II.2 A. *Raba expounded, "What is the meaning of this verse of Scripture: 'Go now and let us reason together, shall the Lord say' (Isa. 1:18)? Instead of 'go' what is required is 'come.'*

B. "In the time to come the Holy One, blessed be He, will say to Israel, 'Go to your fathers and they will rebuke you.'

C. "And they shall say to him, 'Lord of the world, to whom shall we go? Should it be to Abraham, to whom you said, "Know for sure that your seed shall be a stranger...and they shall afflict them..." (Gen. 15:23) — and he didn't seek mercy for us? To Isaac, who blessed Esau, "And it shall come to pass that when you shall have dominion" (Gen. 27:40), and yet he did not seek mercy for us? To Jacob, to whom you said, "I will go down with you to Egypt" (Gen. 46:4), and he didn't ask for mercy for us? So to whom shall we go now? Rather let the Lord say!'

D. "The Holy One, blessed be He, will say to them, 'Since you have thrown yourselves on me, "though your sins be as scarlet, they shall be as white as snow" (Isa. 1:18).'"

II.3 A. *Said R. Samuel bar Nahmani said R. Jonathan, "What is the meaning of the verse of Scripture:* 'For you are our father, though Abraham doesn't know us, and Israel doesn't acknowledge us, you Lord are our father, our redeemer, from everlasting is your name' (Isa. 63:16)?

B. "In the time to come the Holy One, blessed be He, will say to Abraham, 'Your children have sinned against me.' He will answer him, 'Lord of the world, let them be wiped out for the sake of the sanctification of your name.'

C. *"And he will say, 'So I'll go and say this to Jacob, who went through the pain in raising children, maybe he'll ask for mercy for them.'* So he will say to Jacob, 'Your children have sinned against me.' He will answer him, 'Lord of the world, let them be wiped out for the sake of the sanctification of your name.'

D. *"He will say, 'There's no good sense in old men and no good counsel in young ones.'* I'll go tell Isaac, 'Your children have sinned against me.' He will answer him, 'Lord of the world, are they my children and not your children? At the moment when they said to you first '"we will do" and then "we will hearken," you called them "Israel, my son my firstborn" (Ex. 4:22). Now you're calling them my sons, not your sons! And furthermore, how much have they sinned, how many years does a man live? Seventy. *Take off twenty for which you don't impose punishment [Num. 14:29: Those who rejected the gift of the land were punished from twenty years of age and upward], leaving fifty. Take off twenty-five that cover the nights, when people don't sin. Take off twelve and a half for praying, eating, and shitting* — and all you've got is twelve and a half. So if you can take it, well and good, and if not, then let half be on me and half on you And if you should say, they all have to be on me, well, now, I offered myself up to you as a sacrifice.'

E. "They therefore open prayers saying, 'For you are our father.'

F. "Then will Isaac say to them, 'Instead of praising me, praise the Holy One, blessed be He,' *and Isaac will show them the Holy One, blessed be He, with their own eyes.*

G. "On the spot they will raise up their eyes to the heavens and say, 'You Lord are our father our redeemer, from everlasting is your name' (Isa. 63:16)."

[1] Is Moses an active player or a routine and scarcely animate one? The source of energy and the focus of discourse, Moses registers as a critical focus of the revelation of the Torah.

[2] What components of the collection make routine glosses of the received Scriptures and which ones provide more than minor glosses of the tradition? These are not minor glosses but systematic and sustained theology, the center-piece of a sustained narrative.

[3] Can we identify a pronounced bias or a polemical program in the unfolding entries that transform Moses the prophet and king of Israel into Rabbi Moses? Or are the entries that clarify Scripture through the contrast with tradition scattered without pattern in the Rabbinic canon? Moses is a unique figure, contending with the angels and prevailing over them. He is far above sages.

[4] How is Moses comparable to sages in this document? How else may we classify the figure of Moses if not as a sage in this document? He is far above the sages and speaks for all of humanity.

I.43 A. *Our rabbis have taught on Tannaite authority:*
B. What is the order of Mishnah teaching? Moses learned it from the mouth of the All-Powerful. Aaron came in, and Moses repeated his chapter to him and Aaron went forth and sat at the left hand of Moses. His sons came in and Moses repeated their chapter to them, and his sons went forth. Eleazar sat at the right of Moses, and Itamar at the left of Aaron.
C. R. Judah says, "At all times Aaron was at the right hand of Moses."
D. Then the elders entered, and Moses repeated for them their Mishnah chapter. The elders went out. Then the whole people came in, and Moses repeated for them their Mishnah chapter. So it came about that Aaron repeated the lesson four times, his sons three times, the elders two times, and all the people once.
E. Then Moses went out, and Aaron repeated his chapter for them. Aaron went out. His sons repeated their chapter. His sons went out. The elders repeated their chapter. So it turned out that everybody repeated the same chapter four times.
F. On this basis said R. Eliezer, "A person is liable to repeat the lesson for his disciple four times. And it is an argument a fortiori: If Aaron, who studied from Moses himself, and Moses from the Almighty —so in the case of a common person who is studying with a common person, all the more so!"

I.44 A. *So why shouldn't everybody learn directly from Moses?*
B. It was so as to pay honor to Aaron and his sons and honor to the elders.
C. *Then why not have Aaron go in and learn from Moses, then his sons may go in and learn from Aaron, then the elders may go in and learn from his sons, and these in the end will teach all Israel?*
D. Since Moses had learned from the mouth of the All-Powerful, the matter would work out better that way.

I.45 A. The master has said: R. Judah says, "At all times Aaron was at the right hand of Moses" —
B. *In accord with what authority is the following, which has been taught on Tannaite authority:* Three who are going along the way —the master is in the middle, and the more distinguished at the right, the less distinguished on the left? *May we say that this is R. Judah and not rabbis?*

[1] Is Moses an active player or a routine and scarcely animate one? Moses fits a pattern but plays no individual role in that pattern.

[2] What components of the collection make routine glosses of the received Scriptures and which ones provide more than minor glosses of the tradition? The narrative does not gloss scripture.

[3] Can we identify a pronounced bias or a polemical program in the unfolding entries that transform Moses the prophet and king of Israel into Rabbi

Moses? The bias portrays Moses as a sage but a remarkable one because he is disciple to God.

[4] How is Moses comparable to sages in this document? Moses is identical to God's disciple and provides the model of discipleship. How else may we classify the figure of Moses if not as a sage in this document? Moses can be portrayed as conforming to the model of the sage not as a holy man.

21

Moses in Bavli Nashim

BAVLI YEBAMOT 6:6 II.1

H. *So why should the House of Shammai not also derive the governing analogy from the case of Moses?*

I. *They will say to you, "Moses did this only on his own volition." For it has been taught on Tannaite authority:*

J. *There were three things that Moses did only on his own volition, and God concurred with what Moses had decided: going celibate [even without having had a daughter], breaking the tables, and adding one day [to the period of sanctification prior to revelation, Ex. 19:10, 19:15].*

2. A. *"going celibate [even without having had a daughter]:"*

B. *What was the exposition of Scripture that he set forth?*

C. *He thought along these lines: if concerning the Israelites, with whom the Presence of God spoke for only a single moment, and that was at a specified time, the Torah has said, "do not come near a woman," then I, who am singled out for divine speech at any time, and no particular time has been set for me, all the more so should do so — and God concurred with what Moses had decided: "Go say to them, Return you to your tents [wives], but as for you, stand you here by me" (Dt. 5:27-8).*

4. A. *"breaking the tables:"*

B. *What was the exposition of Scripture that he set forth?*

C. *He thought along these lines: if concerning the Passover lamb, only one of six hundred and thirteen commandments, the Torah has said, "No outsider shall eat thereof," then how much the more so should this apply to the whole of the Torah, when all of the Israelites have betrayed it! — and God concurred with what Moses had decided: "which you did break" (Ex. 34:1), concerning which* said R. Simeon b. Laqish, "Said the Holy one blessed be he to Moses, 'Well done for breaking them!'"

4. A. "and adding one day [to the period of sanctification prior to revelation, Ex. 19:10, 19:15]:"
   B. *What was the exposition of Scripture that he set forth?*
   C. *He thought along these lines:* it is written, "And sanctify themselves today and tomorrow" (Ex. 19:10) — today must be like tomorrow. Just as tomorrow means the prior night, so today must encompass the prior night. *But since the prior night applying to today has already gone by, it must follow that there are two days exclusive of today to be observed* — and God concurred with what Moses had decided, *for the Presence of God did not alight before the Sabbath.* [Slotki: the sanctification began on Wednesday, they observed all of Thursday and Friday, and the Presence descended on the Sabbath, the third of the two complete days, as Moses expected, disregarding the first day, which was incomplete].

Moses is an active source of the law. Through his masterful exegesis of the law he guides the unfolding of the law. [1] Moses is an active player and guides the exegetical task through an original reading of Scripture.

[2] What components of the collection make routine glosses of the received Scriptures and which ones provide more than minor glosses of the tradition? The introduction of original readings of Scripture finds the foundations for the propositions that govern.

[3] Moses is not a prophet or a sage but the principal source of the law.

[4] How is Moses comparable to sages in this document? Moses relies on interpretation of Scripture to uncover the law.

III.6

A. Said R. Yosé bar Hanina, "The Torah was given only to Moses and his descendants: 'Write for yourself these words' (Ex. 34:27), and "hew for yourself" (Ex. 34:1). Just as the chips belong to you, so the writing belongs to you. Moses then acted in a generous spirit and gave it to Israel, and in his regard Scripture says, 'A generous person shall be blessed' (Prov. 22:9)."

B. *Objected R. Hisda,* "'And me the Lord commanded at that time to teach you statutes and judgments' (Deut. 4:14)."

C. [By way of reply:] "Me he commanded, and I you."

D. "Behold I have taught you statutes and judgments, even as the Lord my God commanded me" (Deut. 4:15)!

E. [By way of reply:] "Me he commanded, and I you."

F. "Now therefore write this song for you" (Deut. 31:19) [meaning, for the Israelites, not just Moses]!

G. "That speaks only of the song."

21. Moses in Bavli Nashim

H. "That this song be a witness for me against the children of Israel" (Deut. 31:19) [Freedman: if the reference is to the song alone, how can that testify against Israel]?

I. *Only the correct mode of analysis of Scripture was given to Moses alone.*

III.7 A. Said R. Yohanan, "The Holy One, blessed be He, brings his Presence to rest only on a person who is strong, wealthy, wise, and humble, and all of these derive from the example of Moses.

B. "Strong: 'And he spread abroad the tent over the tabernacle' (Ex. 40:19); and a master has said, 'Moses, our Lord, spread it,' and it is written, 'Ten cubits shall be the length of the board' (Ex. 26:16)."

C. *But maybe it was long and thin?*

D. *Proof of his strength derives from this verse:* "And I took the two tablets and cast them out of my two hands and broke them" (Deut. 9:17), *and it was taught on Tannaite authority:* And the tablets were six in length and six in breadth and three thick, lying along the length of the ark.

E. "Wealthy: 'hew for yourself two tablets of stone like the first' (Ex. 34:1) – the chips will belong to you.

F. "Wise:

G. *Both Rab and Samuel say,* "Fifty gates of understanding were created in the world, and all but one of them were given to Moses: 'For you have made Moses a little lower than God' (Ps. 8:6)."

H. "And humble: 'Now the man Moses was very meek' (Num. 12:3)."

III.8 A. Said R. Yohanan, "All of the prophets were wealthy.

B. "How do we know it? From the cases of Moses, Samuel, Amos, and Jonah.

C. "Moses: 'I have not taken one ass from them' (Num. 16:15) – *now if he meant, without paying a fee for its use, then is all that he claimed merely that he wasn't one of those who take without paying a fee? So what he must have meant was, even paying a fee [he had no need to hire animals because he had enough of his own]!"*

D. *But maybe he was too poor to pay a fee for renting an animal?*

E. *Rather, proof derives from* "'hew for yourself two tablets of stone like the first' (Ex. 34:1) – the chips will belong to you.

F. "Samuel: 'Behold, here I am: bear witness against me before the Lord and before his anointed: whose ox have I taken, or whose ass have I taken' (1 Sam. 12:3) – *now if he meant, without paying a fee for its use, then is all that he claimed merely that he wasn't one of those who take without paying a fee? So what he must have meant was, even paying a fee [he had no need to hire animals because he had enough of his own]!"*

G. *But maybe he was too poor to pay a fee for renting an animal?*

H. *Rather, proof derives from* "And his return was to Ramah, for there was his house" (1 Sam. 7:17), on which said Raba, "Wherever he went, his entire retinue went with him."

I. Said Raba, "What is said of Samuel is greater than what is said of Moses. In the case of Moses: 'I have not taken one ass from them' – even for a fee; in the case of Samuel, he did not do so even with their knowledge and consent, 'And they said, you have not defrauded us nor taken advantage of our willingness' (1 Sam. 12:4)."

J. "Amos: 'Then answered Amos and said to Amaziah, I was no prophet nor was I a disciple of a prophet, but I was a herdsman and harvester of sycamore fruit' (Amos 7:14)." *This was translated by R. Joseph, "Behold, I am the owner of flocks and of sycamore trees in the valley."*

K. "Jonah: 'And he found a ship going to Tarshish, so he paid the fare thereof and went down into it' (Jonah 1:3)." And in this connection noted R. Yohanan, "He paid for the rent of the whole ship."

L. R. Romanus said, "The fee to rent the whole ship was four thousand gold denarii."

III.9A. And said R. Yohanan, "To begin with, Moses studied the Torah but forgot it, until it was handed over to him as a gift: 'And he gave unto Moses, when he had made an ending of communing with him...two tablets of testimony' (Ex. 31:18)."

[1] Moses was a central authority of the law through his exegesis of Scripture,

[2] All of the cited exegeses show a dominant role in the law.

[3] Can we identify a pronounced bias in favor of an original reading of the law? Moses reforms the law and sets aside the received text.

[4] How else may we classify the figure of Moses if not as a sage in this document? He can be seen as a sage in the tradition of the Torah, but the tendency throughout is to favor the original reading of Moses.

22

Moses in Bavli Neziqin, Bavli Sanhedrin

BAVLI SANHEDRIN

6:2 I.9 A. Said R. Nahman said Rab, "What is the sense of the verse of Scripture, 'The poor uses entreaties, but the rich answers insolently' (Prov. 18:23)?

B. "'The poor uses entreaties' refers to Moses.

C. "'The rich answers insolently' refers to Joshua."

D. *What is the scriptural basis for that view? Should we say that it is because it is written,* "And they laid them down before the Lord" (Josh. 7:23), R. Nahman said "He came and threw them down before the Lord"?

F. Phineas did it that way, for it is written, "Then Phineas stood up and laid out prayer, and so the plague was stayed" (Ps. 106:30), and R. Eleazar said, "It is not said, 'And he prayed,' but 'And he laid out prayer,' teaching that he behaved contentiously with his creator.

G. "He came and cast [Zimri and Cozbi, Num. 25:7ff.] before the omnipresent, and said before him, 'Lord of the world, on account of these should twenty-four thousand Israelites fall?'

H. "For it is written, 'And those that died by the plague were twenty-four thousand' (Num. 25:9)."

I. *But [it derives] from the following [that Joshua spoke in an insolent way,]* "[And Joshua said, Alas, O Lord,] why have you brought this people over the Jordan" (Josh. 7:7).

J. Moses also spoke in that way, "Why have you dealt ill with this people?" (Ex. 5:22).

K. *Rather, [proof derives] from here:* "Would that we had been content to dwell beyond the Jordan" (Josh. 7:7)!

119

I.10 A. "And the Lord said to Joshua, Get you up" (Josh. 7:10):

B. R. Shila expounded this verse, "Said the Holy one blessed be he to him, 'Your [sin] is more weighty than theirs. For I commanded, "And it shall be when you have passed over the Jordan you shall set up [these stones]" (Deut. 27:4), but you went a distance of sixty miles [to Gerizim and Ebal after crossing the Jordan before setting them up].'"

C. *After he had gone out, Rab appointed an Amora [to deliver his message to those assembled], and interpreted [matters in this way]:* "'As the Lord commanded Moses his servant, so did Moses command Joshua, and so did Joshua; he left nothing undone of all that the Lord had commanded Moses' (Josh. 11:15).

[1] Is Moses an active player or a routine and scarcely animate one? Moses takes an active role in the passage.

[2] What components of the collection make routine glosses of the received Scriptures and which ones provide more than minor glosses of the tradition? Moses makes available a series of minor glosses.

[3] Scripture is illustrated through the contrast with tradition scattered without pattern in the Rabbinic canon?

[4] Moses is a sage in this document.

I.10 A. "And the Lord said to Joshua, Get you up" (Josh. 7:10):

B. R. Shila expounded this verse, "Said the Holy one blessed be he to him, 'Your [sin] is more weighty than theirs. For I commanded, "And it shall be when you have passed over the Jordan you shall set up [these stones]" (Deut. 27:4), but you went a distance of sixty miles [to Gerizim and Ebal after crossing the Jordan before setting them up].'"

C. *After he had gone out, Rab appointed an Amora [to deliver his message to those assembled], and interpreted [matters in this way]:* "'As the Lord commanded Moses his servant, so did Moses command Joshua, and so did Joshua; he left nothing undone of all that the Lord had commanded Moses' (Josh. 11:15).

D. "What then do the words, 'Get you up' (Josh. 7:10) mean?

E. "He said to him, 'You were the one who caused them [to sin]' [Schachter: p. 289, n. 3: by forbidding them the spoil of Jericho].

F. "So [God] said to him in regard to Ai, 'And you shall do to Ai and her king as you did to Jericho and her king, [only the spoil thereof and the cattle thereof shall you take as a prey].' (Josh. 8:2) [But Joshua was not to proclaim a ban of herem on Ai, as he had done on Jericho]."

[1] Moses is a routine and scarcely animate player.
[2] We make routine glosses of the received Scriptures.'

[3] The entries that clarify Scripture through the contrast with tradition are scattered without pattern in the Rabbinic canon?

[4] Moses is comparable to sages in this document.

23

Moses in Bavli Qodoshim and Niddah

BAVLI MENAHOT CHAPTER ELEVEN

2. A. *There we have learned in the Mishnah:*
   B. **When Yosé b. Yoezer of Seredah and Yosé b. Yohanan of Jerusalem died, the grape-clusters were ended, since it is said, "There is no cluster to eat, my soul desires the first ripe fig" (Micah 7:1) [M. Sot. 9:9E-F].**
   C. What is the meaning of "grape-clusters"? It means, "a man in whom all things are to be found" [the Hebrew letters of the word for grape cluster yielding such a meaning].
   D. And said R. Judah said Samuel, "All the grape-clusters who arose for Israel from the time of Moses until Joseph ben Yoezer died learned the Torah like Moses, our master. From that time onward, they did not learn the Torah like Moses our master."
   E. But did not R. Judah say Samuel said, "Three thousand laws were forgotten during the period of mourning for Moses"?
   F. *The ones that were forgotten were indeed forgotten, but as to the ones that people did learn, they learned them as did Moses, our master.*
   G. *But has it not been taught on Tannaite authority:*
   H. Once Moses died, if those who declared an object susceptible to uncleanness, it was declared unclean, if those who declared it insusceptible to uncleanness formed the majority, it was declared insusceptible.
   I. *It is their heart that diminished, but their learning went on like the learning of Moses, our master.*
3. A. *A Tannaite authority has taught:*
   B. In none of the grape-clusters that arose for Israel from the time of Moses until Joseph b. Yoezer of Seredah died was found no flaw.

From that time onward, there were flaws in them.
- C. *But has it not been taught on Tannaite authority:*
- D. There is the case of a certain pious man, who groaned because of heartburn, and they asked the physicians, who said, "There is no remedy unless he drink hot milk from a goat morning by morning." So they brought a goat and tied it to the foot of his bed, and he would suck hot milk from it.
- E. Some time later his friends came to visit him. When they saw the goat [a small beast, which it is forbidden to keep in the Land of Israel], they said, "Armed robbers are in his house, and are we going to visit him?"
- F. [When he died,] they went into session and the examined his case and found that that sin involving the goat was the only sin that pertained to him. He too, when he was dying, said, "I know in my own regard that that sin involving the goat was the only sin that pertained to me, for in that case I violated the teachings of my colleagues. For sages have taught, 'People are not to raise small cattle in the Land of Israel.'"
- G *Now it is an established fact that when we find a reference to "a certain pious man," it is either R. Judah b. Baba or R. Judah bar Ilai. Now these rabbis lived many generations after Joseph b. Yoezer of Seredah [and the text is explicit that they were unblemished]!*
- H. [16A] Said R. Joseph, "The flaw concerns disputes, e.g., a dispute concerning the laying on of hands [but prior to that dispute, recorded at M. Hag. 2:2, there was no dispute]."
- I. *But Yosé b. Yoezer himself is involved in that dispute concerning the laying on of hands?*
- J. *When he participated in the dispute, it was when he had come to the end of his years, at which time his heart was straitened."*

We now revert to I:2C and clarify that matter. The composite that follows clearly was formed in its own framework and inserted here for the explicitly-stated reason.

- 4. A. *Reverting to the text just now cited:*
  - B. R. Judah said Samuel said, "Three thousand laws were forgotten during the period of mourning for Moses."
  - C. They said to Joshua, "Ask."
  - D. He said to them, "'It is not in Heaven' (Dt. 30:12)."
  - E. They said to Samuel, "Ask."
  - F. He said to them, "'These are the commandments' (Num. 36:13) — for a prophet [such as myself] has not got the right to innovate in any way from now on."
- 5. A. Said Isaac the smith, "Also the law on the disposition of a sin offering, the owner of which has day, was forgotten in the time of mourning for Moses."

- B. They said to Phineas, "Ask."
- C. He said to them, "'It is not in Heaven' (Dt. 30:12)."
- E. They said to Eleazar, "Ask."
- F. He said to them, "'These are the commandments' (Num. 36:13) — for a prophet has not got the right to innovate in any way from now on."

6. A. Said R. Judah said Rab, "When Moses, our master, was taking leave for the Garden of Eden, he said to Joshua, 'Ask me any doubts that you have.'
- B. "He said to him, 'My master, have I ever left you, even for a single moment, and gone somewhere else? Did you not write concerning me, "But his servant Joshua the son of Nun did not depart from the tabernacle" (Ex 33:11)?'
- C. "Forthwith Joshua grew weak, and he forgot three hundred laws, and seven hundred doubts were born in his mind, and all of Israel arose to kill him. Said the Holy One, blessed be he, to him, 'To tell you [what you have forgotten] is no longer possible, but go and preoccupy them with a patriotic war.' For it is said, 'Now after the death of Moses, servant of the Lord, it came to pass that the Lord spoke' (Josh. 1:1) and further, 'Prepare food, for within three days...' (Josh. 1:11)."

7. A. *In a Tannaite tradition it is taught:*
- B. A thousand and seven hundred arguments a fortiori and arguments by analogy and scribal clarifications were forgotten in the time of the mourning for Moses.
- C. Said R. Abbahu, "Nonetheless, Othniel b. Kenaz restored them by means of his sharp wit: 'And Othniel son of Kenaz the brother of Caleb took it [the city of the book]' (Josh. 15:17)."

The next set forms a systematic exposition of Josh. 15:17ff.

8. A. "and he gave him Achsah his daughter to wife" (Josh. 15:17):
- D. Why was she called "Achsah"?
- E. Said R. Yohanan, "Because whoever saw her became dissatisfied with his wife.

9. A. "When she came to him she urged him to ask her father for a field, and she alighted from her ass" (Josh. 15:17-19):
- B. *What is the meaning of the word translated* "alighted"?
- C. Said Raba said R. Isaac, "She said to him, 'Just as, when this ass has no food in its crib, it forthwith cries out, so a woman, when she has no food in her house, forthwith cries out."

10. A. "and Caleb said to her, 'What do you want?' She said to him, 'Give me a present, since you have set me in the land of the Negeb" (Josh. 15:17-19):
- B. "It is a house that is dry of all good [that you have given me]."
- C. "'give me also springs of water.' [This refers to] a man who has only Torah alone in him."

11. A. "And Caleb gave her the upper springs and the lower springs" (Josh. 15:17-19):

B. He said to her, "From him to whom all the secrets of the upper world and the nether world are revealed, ask food from him."

12. A. Now was Caleb the son of Kenaz ["And Othniel son of Kenaz the brother of Caleb took it [the city of the book]" (Josh. 15:17)]? Was Caleb not the son of Jephunneh?

B. The meaning of the word Jephunneh is that he turned away from the advice of the spies [since the word "turn away from" shares consonants with the name Jephunneh].

C. Still, was Caleb the son of Kenaz? He was the son of Hezron: "And Caleb the son of Hezron begat Azubah" (1 Chr. 2:18).

D. *Said Raba, "He was the step-son of Kenaz"*

[1] Moses is scarcely animate. He marks time differences. [2] Moses supplies little more than minor glosses of the tradition.

[3] The entries are scattered without pattern in the Rabbinic canon.

[4] We classify the figure of Moses as a sage in this document.

24

Moses as a Figure in the Documentary Catalogue

Two types of writing encompass the random collections of Rabbi Moses: [1] active exegete of Scripture and [2] passive topic comprised by random narratives of sages' learning and virtue. My account of the traits of the documentary traditions of Rabbi Moses accordingly divides into two types of writing, NARRATIVE of Moses as exemplary rabbi and EXEGESIS of Scripture by Moses. Moses is an active figure in the category of exegesis and is a passive category in the narratives.

What is at stake in the present characterization of the documents of Scripture and the Rabbinic canon? We ask whether the documents in which Moses figures coalesce and form a coherent statement. We want to know how the Mishnah portrays Moses and how the scriptural Isaiah sees him — and on through the canon.

We look in vain for documentary lines of differentiation. This observation is meant to answer the question, was there a tradition of Rabbi Moses and where in the documentary heritage of Rabbinic Judaism do we find it? The answer is partly positive in that we can identify the theological propositions of most of the documents one by one. And it is partly negative in that we locate in the documents no resort to traditions of particular rabbis and their viewpoints. The upshot is simply stated. There was no biographical program distinctive to the canon produced by sages. The documents are distinguished from one another by striking qualities of theological differentiation, but these do not encompass the forms that guided us in our documentary inquiry. Let us survey the canon of the rabbis.

1. MOSES IN THE MISHNAH AND ABOT

The Mishnah does not assemble large collections of stories about rabbis. It does put together a few anecdotal stories but these do not pretend to tell a life story of holy men, whether sage or prophet. The Mishnah situates Moses on lists of authorities in the effort to include Moses on lists of sages-saints. What defines Moses above all is the phrase "the law [given] to Moses on Sinai." Moses is a link in the chain of tradition of Sinai.

In Abot Moses is the model of the sage. But Moses is one among several figures on common lists, an unimportant figure, and he does not engage with the stories about Rabbi Moses, He is portrayed as a sage among sages, and little else,

2. MOSES IN THE TOSEFTA

Moses is exemplary and is cited as the model for Israelite conduct. Unlike the collection in Mishnah and Abot, Tosefta Sotah tells an elaborate biographical story. It concerns how Moses showed his virtue in burying Joseph. The story contains minor supernatural elements. Moses is an example of virtue. But he is not a principal holy man.

3. MOSES IN SIFRA

Moses is skilled at interpreting God's messages. There is little beyond formal exegesis. The figure of Moses makes no distinctive impression.

4. MOSES IN SIFRE TO NUMBERS AND SIFRE ZUTTA TO NUMBERS

Moses contributes several exegetical exercises, following the model of citation of Scripture jammed to the eisegesis of Scripture and a phrase that responded.

5. MOSES IN SIFRÉ TO DEUTERONOMY

Moses is a fully exposed personality and subject of a complex narrative. Moses is a model of virtue and is part of the prophetic circle. But even here Moses is not subject of a fully exposed biography. Sifre to Deuteronomy provides large segments of a life. This is the earliest-redacted collection of narrative anecdotes,

6. MOSES IN MEKHILTA ATTRIBUTED TO R. ISHMAEL

Mekhilta Attributed to R. Ishmael is the first document in the Rabbinic achieve to introduce a clear parable, the first narrative collection in the Rabbinic canon to require a parable.

7. MOSES IN GENESIS RABBAH

Moses occurs casually, and the document does not focus on his life and acts. There is no focus for the stories about Moses. I cannot encompass Genesis Rabbah in the classification and repertoire of writings, whether narrative of exegetical.

8. MOSES IN LEVITICUS RABBAH

A parable provides the program for Moses in Leviticus. Moses is not unique. He is not exposed as a principal figure. Moses is portrayed as comparable to a prophet.

9. MOSES IN PESIQTA DERAB KAHANA

Three cases in which God's requirements are shown to be moderate indeed, scarcely commensurate to God's glory. No. 7 then goes over the same matter. "There were three statements that Moses heard from the mouth of the Almighty, on account of which he was astounded and recoiled." Moses is a sage advocating a reasonable program of interpretation of Scripture.

10. MOSES IN ESTHER RABBAH I

Moses is no different from other holy men.

11. MOSES IN SONG OF SONGS RABBAH

Moses is assigned minor glosses and contributes simple comments.

12. MOSES IN RUTH RABBAH

Moses is a routine figure and glosses involving him are scarce. He is not comparable to sages in this document.

13. MOSES IN LAMENTATIONS RABBAH

Moses mourns for Israel's fate. He is comparable to any one of the fathers. He is not a unique figure but a familiar one.

14. MOSES IN THE FATHERS ACCORDING TO RABBI NATHAN

Moses is a highly active figure. He takes up the prophetic charge and is characterized as our master, the sage, the greatest of the great. Moses is a coherent figure and is a model for Rabbinic conduct.

15 MOSES IN YERUSHALMI BERAKHOT AND ZERAIM

The Gemara or Talmud supplies narratives of Moses but does not adhere to a model that governs the document as a whole. I find no large scale conception that provides rules for documentary traits overall,

16. MOSES IN YERUSHALMI MOED

Moses is source of routine exegeses of Scripture and is himself a standard sage.

17. MOSES IN YERUSHALMI NASHIM

Moses yields no consequential compositions or composites in Yerushalmi Nashim.

18. MOSES IN YERUSHALMI NEZIQIN

Moses is not stymied by challenges to the logic of the law.

19. MOSES IN BAVLI BREAKHOT

We have a sequence of incoherent composites, Moses is just another sage.

20. MOSES IN BAVLI MOED

Moses can be portrayed as conforming to the model of the sage not as a holy man.

21. MOSES IN BAVLI NASHIM

Moses is primarily an exegete of Scripture, and that is what marks him as a principal source of the Torah. Moses can be seen as a sage in the tradition of the Torah, but the tendency throughout is to favor the original reading of Moses.

22. MOSES IN BAVLI NEZIQIN

We make routine glosses of the received Scriptures. The entries that clarify Scripture through the contrast with tradition are scattered without pattern in the Rabbinic canon.

23 MOSES IN BAVLI QODOSHIM AND NIDDAH

The entries are scattered without pattern in the Rabbinic canon.

24. CONCLUSION. MOSES AS A FIGURE IN THE DOCUMENTARY CATALOGUE

We find in the Rabbinic collections no evidence of the presence of a coherent biography or tradition that is even connected with the figure of Moses. Moses appears in two forms, as a sage and as a prophet. There are anecdotes but few literary tendencies connected with him. Rabbi Moses touches on odds and ends but points to no program that covers the whole picture. What then do we find? Moses fits *ab initio* with the tradition of rabbis serving as exegetes. Moses as exegete dominates.

The Rabbinic documents on which we have had to rely are collections of propositions put forth by sages engaged in exegesis and that is how they relate to rabbis as well. If we review the survey we have constructed we find that one result. The initial story of Rabbi Moses concerns the burial of Joseph by Moses and provides an elaborate narrative of Moses.

The portrait of Rabbi Moses by the successive documents does not provide for large collections of stories but does take account of the two strands of the tradition-narratives of Moses and exegetes of scripture. It is now our task to summarize our results for the documentary hypothesis.

The documents in which the figure of Moses portrayed as a sage, the narrative of the sages' virtue

    MOSES IN THE MISHNAH AND ABOT
    MOSES IN THE TOSEFTA
    MOSES IN SIFRÉ TO DEUTERONOMY
    MOSES IN MEKHILTA ATTRIBUTED TO R. ISHMAEL
    MOSES IN LEVITICUS RABBAH
    MOSES IN PESIQTA DERAB KAHANA
    MOSES IN ESTHER RABBAH I
    MOSES IN LAMENTATIONS RABBAH
    MOSES IN THE FATHERS ACCORDING TO RABBI NATHAN

The documents in which the figure of Moses dominates as an exegete of Scripture:
    MOSES IN THE TOSEFTA

MOSES IN SIFRE TO NUMBERS AND SIFRE ZUTTA TO NUMBERS
MOSES IN SONG OF SONGS RABBAH
MOSES IN RUTH RABBAH
MOSES IN YERUSHALMI NEZIQIN
MOSES IN YERUSHALMI MOED
MOSES IN BAVLI NEZIQIN
MOSES IN BAVLI NASHIM

Considering the traits of comprehensive documents yields a random sample of this and that. I discern no correlation between the documents and their paramount traits — those of sages or of exegetes. We are able to sort out the Rabbinic documents by appeal to their preferences of form and to theological or Halakhic concerns. But when we pay attention to the documents' boundaries, we see no paramount patterns. Indeed, no dominant patterns emerge in response to the documentary differentiation. That produces a puzzle for the documentary hypothesis, with its heavy emphasis on the formal differentiation between or among documents. The figure of Rabbi Moses has no foundations in the canonical collections. He is a figment of the imaginative construction of random exegetes and makes collections of occasional tales.

What is missing? What the collection of Rabbinic documents lack is a focus, coherence, a proposition at the heart of matters — and that is at the deepest level of analysis. The documents offer no picture of the man and his entire way of life and cogent system. The figure of Rabbi Moses never serves to join together the entire corpus or any substantial part of it.

The upshot is now clear. Rabbinic Judaism possessed no vision of biography and makes no provision for a biographical category. It ignored the options exercised by other contemporary systems. That is why we find little more than remnants of biographical or programmatic interest. The canon knows two categorical aspects of large-scale experience: exegesis of scripture and narrative of anecdotes —which are two examples of the same thing: illustration of a few rules. The case of biography presents no anomaly but only an example. What we learn from Rabbi Moses we can learn from any other rabbi. And that is that sages reliably interpret Scripture.

That result is hardly surprising, but it does register a fundamental point. The documents of Rabbinic Judaism conform to other observed traits of that Judaism, which treat the Torah as an exegetical focus and the exemplary character of sages as a subordinate locus. The absence of large scale statements attests to the character of the Rabbinic system. It makes large-scale statements about Scripture and only in a subordinate role does the system register its main points.

That observation of the anecdotal character of the Rabbinic writings underscores the striking categorical contrast between the Torah and the Gospels. There we are struck by a recurrent pattern. It is the one yielded by the extended biography of Jesus in comparison with the anecdotal exercise of the sages. But both sources of biographical assertion — the Rabbinic canon and the Gospels narratives — contrast with the letters of Paul, with their utter disinterest in personal data whether anecdotal or systematic.

STUDIES IN JUDAISM
TITLES IN THE SERIES
PUBLISHED BY UNIVERSITY PRESS OF AMERICA

Judith Z. Abrams
The Babylonian Talmud: A Topical Guide, 2002.

Roger David Aus
The Death, Burial, and Resurrection of Jesus, and the Death, Burial, and Translation of Moses in Judaic Tradition, 2008.

Feeding the Five Thousand: Studies in the Judaic Background of Mark 6:30-44 par. and John 6:1-15, 2010.

Matthew 1-2 and the Virginal Conception: In Light of Palestinian and Hellenistic Judaic Traditions on the Birth of Israel's First Redeemer, Moses, 2004.

My Name Is "Legion": Palestinian Judaic Traditions in Mark 5:1-20 and Other Gospel Texts, 2003.

Simon Peter's Denial and Jesus' Commissioning Him as His Successor in John 21:15–19: Studies in Their Judaic Background, 2013.

Alan L. Berger, Harry James Cargas, and Susan E. Nowak
The Continuing Agony: From the Carmelite Convent to the Crosses at Auschwitz, 2004.

S. Daniel Breslauer
Creating a Judaism without Religion: A Postmodern Jewish Possibility, 2001.

Bruce Chilton
Targumic Approaches to the Gospels: Essays in the Mutual Definition of Judaism and Christianity, 1986.

David Ellenson
Tradition in Transition: Orthodoxy, Halakhah, and the Boundaries of Modern Jewish Identity, 1989.

Roberta Rosenberg Farber and Simcha Fishbane
Jewish Studies in Violence: A Collection of Essays, 2007.

Paul V. M. Flesher
New Perspectives on Ancient Judaism, Volume 5: Society and Literature in Analysis, 1990.

Marvin Fox
Collected Essays on Philosophy and on Judaism, Volume One: Greek Philosophy, Maimonides, 2003.

Collected Essays on Philosophy and on Judaism, Volume Two: Some Philosophers, 2003.

Collected Essays on Philosophy and on Judaism, Volume Three: Ethics, Reflections, 2003.

Zev Garber
Methodology in the Academic Teaching of Judaism, 1986.

Zev Garber, Alan L. Berger, and Richard Libowitz
Methodology in the Academic Teaching of the Holocaust, 1988.

Abraham Gross
Spirituality and Law: Courting Martyrdom in Christianity and Judaism, 2005.

Harold S. Himmelfarb and Sergio DellaPergola
Jewish Education Worldwide: Cross-Cultural Perspectives, 1989.

Luise Hirsch
From the Shtetl to the Lecture Hall: Jewish Women and Cultural Exchange, 2012.

Raphael Jospe
Jewish Philosophy: Foundations and Extensions (Volume One: General Questions and Considerations), 2008.

Jewish Philosophy: Foundations and Extensions (Volume Two: On Philosophers and Their Thought), 2008.

William Kluback
The Idea of Humanity: Hermann Cohen's Legacy to Philosophy and Theology, 1987.

Samuel Morell
Studies in the Judicial Methodology of Rabbi David ibn Abi Zimra, 2004.

Jacob Neusner
Amos in Talmud and Midrash, 2006.

Analytical Templates of the Yerushalmi, 2008.

Ancient Israel, Judaism, and Christianity in Contemporary Perspective, 2006.

The Aggadic Role in Halakhic Discourses: Volume I, 2001.

The Aggadic Role in Halakhic Discourses: Volume II, 2001.

The Aggadic Role in Halakhic Discourses: Volume III, 2001.

Analysis and Argumentation in Rabbinic Judaism, 2003.

Analytical Templates of the Bavli, 2006.

Ancient Judaism and Modern Category-Formation: "Judaism," "Midrash," "Messianism," and Canon in the Past Quarter Century, 1986.

Bologna Addresses and Other Recent Papers, 2007.

Building Blocks of Rabbinic Tradition: The Documentary Approach to the Study of Formative Judaism, 2007.

Canon and Connection: Intertextuality in Judaism, 1987.

Chapters in the Formative History of Judaism, 2006.

Chapters in the Formative History of Judaism: Second Series: More Questions and Answers, 2008.

Chapters in the Formative History of Judaism: Third Series: Historical Theology, the Canon, Constructive Theology and Other Problems, 2009.

Chapters in the Formative History of Judaism: Fourth Series: From-Historical Studies and the Documentary Hypothesis, 2009.

Chapters in the Formative History of Judaism: Fifth Series: Some Current Essays on the History, Literature, and Theology of Judaism, 2010.

Chapters in the Formative History of Judaism: Sixth Series: More Essays on the History, Literature, and Theology of Judaism, 2011.

Chapters in the Formative History of Judaism: Seventh Series: More Essays on the History, Literature, and Theology of Judaism, 2011.

Chapters in the Formative History of Judaism: Eighth Series: Systemic Perspectives, 2012.

Comparative Midrash: Sifré to Numbers and Sifré Zutta to Numbers: Two Rabbinic Readings of the Book of Numbers, Volume One: Forms, 2009.

Comparative Midrash: Sifré to Numbers and Sifré Zutta to Numbers: Two Rabbinic Readings of the Book of Numbers, Volume Two: Exegesis, 2009.

The Documentary History of Judaism and Its Recent Interpreters, 2009

Dual Discourse, Single Judaism, 2001.

The Emergence of Judaism: Jewish Religion in Response to the Critical Issues of the First Six Centuries, 2000.

Ezekiel in Talmud and Midrash, 2007.

First Principles of Systemic Analysis: The Case of Judaism within the History of Religion, 1988.

First Steps in the Talmud: A Guide to the Confused, 2010.

Habakkuk, Jonah, Nahum, and Obadiah in Talmud and Midrash: A Source Book, 2007.

The Halakhah and the Aggadah, 2001.

Halakhic Hermeneutics, 2003.

Halakhic Theology: A Sourcebook, 2006.

The Hermeneutics of Rabbinic Category Formations, 2001.

Hosea in Talmud and Midrash, 2006.

How Important Was the Destruction of the Second Temple in the Formation of Rabbinic Judaism? 2006.

How Not to Study Judaism, Examples and Counter-Examples, Volume One: Parables, Rabbinic Narratives, Rabbis' Biographies, Rabbis' Disputes, 2004.

How Not to Study Judaism, Examples and Counter-Examples, Volume Two: Ethnicity and Identity Versus Culture and Religion, How Not to Write a Book on Judaism, Point and Counterpoint, 2004.

How the Bavli is Constructed: Identifying the Forests Comprised by the Talmud's Trees: The Cases of Bavli Moed Qatan and of Bavli Makkot, 2009.

How the Halakhah Unfolds: Moed Qatan in the Mishnah, Tosefta, Yerushalmi, and Bavli, 2006.

How the Halakhah Unfolds, Volume II, Part A: Nazir in the Mishnah, Tosefta, Yerushalmi, and Bavli, 2007.

How the Halakhah Unfolds, Volume II, Part B: Nazir in the Mishnah, Tosefta, Yerushalmi, and Bavli, 2007.

How the Halakhah Unfolds, Volume III, Part A: Abodah Zarah in the Mishnah, Tosefta, Yerushalmi, and Bavli, 2007.

How the Halakhah Unfolds, Volume III, Part B: Abodah Zarah in the Mishnah, Tosefta, Yerushalmi, and Bavli, 2007.

How the Halakhah Unfolds, Volume IV, Hagigah in the Mishnah, Tosefta, Yerushalmi, and Bavli, 2009.

The Implicit Norms of Rabbinic Judaism, 2006.

Intellectual Templates of the Law of Judaism, 2006.

Isaiah in Talmud and Midrash: A Source Book, Part A, 2007.

Isaiah in Talmud and Midrash: A Source Book, Part B, 2007.

Is Scripture the Origin of the Halakhah? 2005

Israel and Iran in Talmudic Times: A Political History, 1986.

Israel's Politics in Sasanian Iran: Self-Government in Talmudic Times, 1986.

Jeremiah in Talmud and Midrash: A Source Book, 2006.

Judaism in Monologue and Dialogue, 2005.

Lost Documents of Rabbinic Judaism. 2010.

Major Trends in Formative Judaism, Fourth Series, 2002.

Major Trends in Formative Judaism, Fifth Series, 2002.

Messiah in Context: Israel's History and Destiny in Formative Judaism, 1988.

Micah and Joel in Talmud and Midrash, 2006.

Narrative and Document in the Rabbinic Canon, Vol. I: From the Mishnah to the Talmuds, 2009.

Narrative and Document in the Rabbinic Canon, Vol. II: The Two Talmuds, 2010.

The Native Category – Formations of the Aggadah: The Later Midrash-Compilations – Volume I, 2000.

The Native Category – Formations of the Aggadah: The Earlier Midrash-Compilations – Volume II, 2000.

Paradigms in Passage: Patterns of Change in the Contemporary Study of Judaism, 1988.

Parsing the Torah, 2005.

Persia and Rome in Classical Judaism, 2008

Praxis and Parable: The Divergent Discourses of Rabbinic Judaism, 2006.

The Program of the Fathers According to Rabbi Nathan A, 2009.

Rabbi David: A Documentary Catalogue, 2012.

Rabbi Jeremiah, 2006.

Rabbi Moses: A Documentary Catalogue, 2013.

The Rabbinic System: How the Aggadah and the Halakhah Complement Each Other, 2011.

Rabbinic Theology and Israelite Prophecy: Primacy of the Torah, Narrative of the World to Come, Doctrine of Repentance and Atonement, and the Systematization of Theology in the Rabbis' Reading of the Prophets, 2007.

The Rabbinic Utopia, 2007.

The Rabbis and the Prophets, 2010.

The Rabbis, the Law, and the Prophets. 2007.

Reading Scripture with the Rabbis: The Five Books of Moses, 2006.

The Religious Study of Judaism: Description, Analysis, Interpretation, Volume 1, 1986.

The Religious Study of Judaism: Description, Analysis, Interpretation, Volume 2, 1986.

The Religious Study of Judaism: Context, Text, Circumstance, Volume 3, 1987.

The Religious Study of Judaism: Description, Analysis, Interpretation, Volume 4, 1988.

Sifré Zutta to Numbers, 2008.

Struggle for the Jewish Mind: Debates and Disputes on Judaism Then and Now, 1988.

The Talmud Law, Theology, Narrative: A Sourcebook, 2005.

Talmud Torah: Ways to God's Presence through Learning: An Exercise in Practical Theology, 2002.

Texts Without Boundaries: Protocols of Non-Documentary Writing in the Rabbinic Canon: Volume I: The Mishnah, Tractate Abot, and the Tosefta, 2002.

Texts Without Boundaries: Protocols of Non-Documentary Writing in the Rabbinic Canon: Volume II: Sifra and Sifre to Numbers, 2002.

Texts Without Boundaries: Protocols of Non-Documentary Writing in the Rabbinic Canon: Volume III: Sifre to Deuteronomy and Mekhilta Attributed to Rabbi Ishmael, 2002.

Texts Without Boundaries: Protocols of Non-Documentary Writing in the Rabbinic Canon: Volume IV: Leviticus Rabbah, 2002.

A Theological Commentary to the Midrash – Volume I: Pesiqta deRab Kahana, 2001.

A Theological Commentary to the Midrash – Volume II: Genesis Raba, 2001.

A Theological Commentary to the Midrash – Volume III: Song of Songs Rabbah, 2001.

A Theological Commentary to the Midrash – Volume IV: Leviticus Rabbah, 2001.

A Theological Commentary to the Midrash – Volume V: Lamentations Rabbati, 2001.

A Theological Commentary to the Midrash – Volume VI: Ruth Rabbah and Esther Rabbah, 2001.

A Theological Commentary to the Midrash – Volume VII: Sifra, 2001.

A Theological Commentary to the Midrash – Volume VIII: Sifre to Numbers and Sifre to Deuteronomy, 2001.

A Theological Commentary to the Midrash – Volume IX: Mekhilta Attributed to Rabbi Ishmael, 2001.

Theological Dictionary of Rabbinic Judaism: Part One: Principal Theological Categories, 2005.

Theological Dictionary of Rabbinic Judaism: Part Two: Making Connections and Building Constructions, 2005.

Theological Dictionary of Rabbinic Judaism: Part Three: Models of Analysis, Explanation, and Anticipation, 2005.

The Theological Foundations of Rabbinic Midrash, 2006.

Theology of Normative Judaism: A Source Book, 2005.

Theology in Action: How the Rabbis of the Talmud Present Theology (Aggadah) in the Medium of the Law (Halakhah). An Anthology, 2006.

The Torah and the Halakhah: The Four Relationships, 2003.

The Transformation of Judaism: From Philosophy to Religion, Second Edition, Revised, 2010.

The Treasury of Judaism: A New Collection and Translation of Essential Texts (Volume One: The Calendar), 2008.

The Treasury of Judaism: A New Collection and Translation of Essential Texts (Volume Two: The Life Cycle), 2008.

The Treasury of Judaism: A New Collection and Translation of Essential Texts (Volume Three: Theology), 2008.

The Unity of Rabbinic Discourse: Volume I: Aggadah in the Halakhah, 2001.

The Unity of Rabbinic Discourse: Volume II: Halakhah in the Aggadah, 2001.

The Unity of Rabbinic Discourse: Volume III: Halakhah and Aggadah in Concert, 2001.

The Vitality of Rabbinic Imagination: The Mishnah Against the Bible and Qumran, 2005.

War and Peace in Rabbinic Judaism: A Documentary Account, 2011.

Who, Where and What is "Israel?": Zionist Perspectives on Israeli and American Judaism, 1989.

The Wonder-Working Lawyers of Talmudic Babylonia: The Theory and Practice of Judaism in its Formative Age, 1987.

Zephaniah, Haggai, Zechariah, and Malachi in Talmud and Midrash: A Source Book, 2007.

Jacob Neusner and Renest S. Frerichs
New Perspectives on Ancient Judaism, Volume 2: Judaic and Christian Interpretation of Texts: Contents and Contexts, 1987.

New Perspectives on Ancient Judaism, Volume 3: Judaic and Christian Interpretation of Texts: Contents and Contexts, 1987

Jacob Neusner and James F. Strange
Religious Texts and Material Contexts, 2001.

David Novak and Norbert M. Samuelson
Creation and the End of Days: Judaism and Scientific Cosmology, 1986.

Proceedings of the Academy for Jewish Philosophy, 1990.

Risto Nurmela
The Mouth of the Lord Has Spoken: Inner-Biblical Allusions in Second and Third Isaiah, 2006.

Aaron D. Panken
The Rhetoric of Innovation: Self-Conscious Legal Change in Rabbinic Literature, 2005.

Norbert M. Samuelson
Studies in Jewish Philosophy: Collected Essays of the Academy for Jewish Philosophy, 1980-1985, 1987.

Benjamin Edidin Scolnic
Alcimus, Enemy of the Maccabees, 2004.

If the Egyptians Drowned in the Red Sea, Where Are the Pharoah's Chariots?: Exploring the Historical Dimension of the Bible, 2005.

Judaism Defined: Mattathias and the Destiny of His People. 2010.

Thy Brother's Blood: The Maccabees and Dynastic Morality in the Hellenistic World, 2008.

Rivka Ulmer

Pesiqta Rabbati: A Synoptic Edition of Pesiqta Rabbati Based Upon All Extant Manuscripts and the Editio Preceps, Volume I, 2009.

Pesiqta Rabbati: A Synoptic Edition of Pesiqta Rabbati Based Upon All Extant Manuscripts and the Editio Preceps, Volume II, 2009.

Pesiqta Rabbati: A Synoptic Edition of Pesiqta Rabbati Based Upon All Extant Manuscripts and the Editio Preceps, Volume III, 2009.

Manfred Vogel

A Quest for a Theology of Judaism: The Divine, the Human and the Ethical Dimensions in the Structure-of-Faith of Judaism Essays in Constructive Theology, 1987.

Anita Weiner

Renewal: Reconnecting Soviet Jewry to the Soviet People: A Decade of American Jewish Joint Distribution Committee (AJJDC) Activities in the Former Soviet Union 1988-1998, 2003.

Eugene Weiner and Anita Weiner

Israel-A Precarious Sanctuary: War, Death and the Jewish People, 1989.

The Martyr's Conviction: A Sociological Analysis, 2002.

Leslie S. Wilson

The Serpent Symbol in the Ancient Near East: Nahash and Asherah: Death, Life, and Healing, 2001.

Tzvee Zahavy and Jacob Neusner

How the Halakhah Unfolds, Volume V: Hullin in the Mishnah, Tosefta, and Bavli, Part One: Mishnah, Tosefta, and Bavli, Chapters One through Six, 2010.

How the Halakhah Unfolds, Volume V: Hullin in the Mishnah, Tosefta and Bavli, Part Two: Mishnah, Tosefta, and Bavli, Chapters Seven through Twelve, 2010.